BREAK the LINE

Analysis & Method in Attacking Rugby

SECOND EDITION

RICK FERRARA
WITH
PHIL SHARPE

All rights reserved. No part of this publication may be reproduced, stored in a retrieval system, or transmitted in any form or by any means, electronic, mechanical, photocopying, recording or otherwise, without the prior written permission of the Author and Publisher.

ISBN: 978-0-578-36833-7

All content within this book, including the words and diagrams, is authored by and with exclusive copyright to Rick L. Ferrara of Cleveland, Ohio, USA, 2022 ©

Cover photo is courtesy of t-fizzle photography, Cleveland, Ohio at Tfizzlephotography.com, and featuring Kevin McLaughlin of the Cleveland Rovers and Taryn Avon of the Cleveland Crusaders.

Break the Line: Second Edition ("Break the Line") is Published by Rick L. Ferrara, 2077 E. 4th Street, 2nd Floor, Cleveland, Ohio, 44115 and via Amazon.com.

Follow Break the Line on Twitter and Instagram: @BTLRugby

QR codes herein link to outside websites preselected by the author, are for reference only, are accessible publicly, and are not affiliated with the author or publisher of this book. Break the Line suggests no copyright ownership to the images, players, likenesses, music, commentary, or broadcasts shown at the link locations.

Further, Break the Line is neither endorsed by, in partnership with, nor has any affiliation with any of the teams, organizations, or companies shown in the links provided, including World Rugby or any of the teams, players, or corporations portrayed in the links unless otherwise noted. The links are provided for educational reference only.

The links may, due to YouTube's monetized design, include advertisements. Break the Line neither regulates the content of those advertisements nor profits from them.

Second Edition layout designed by Simon Thompson, who can be found on Instagram @alteredimagesdesign

Notes to Readers: Learn rugby with a coach. Play safe. The author has worked diligently to make sure the concepts herein are technically accurate. However, neither the author nor the publisher can accept responsibility for any injury or loss sustained a result of the use of this material.

Acknowledgements and Thanks...

 My rugby career started the night I watched a video of my friend Jeff playing rugby at Ashland University. When my next college semester started, I attended the next club practice and never looked back.

Thank you to my rugby brethren, starting with my first coach at Marquette University, Boris Turcinovic, to whom I owe a great deal, my first backline coach Yan, and teammates from Marquette University, especially my lifelong friends Alejandro, Paddy, and England. Thanks go to Chin and Big Wally for providing my first coaching experience and being such good men, and to all the Homestead Highlanders and their families for their support, commitment, and friendship.

Thanks to all my Cleveland Rovers teammates, especially Craig for the intro to the team and his brotherhood, and Dale, Paul, Dave, and Sean for their leadership and guidance. Thanks goes to Matt and Jason for giving me my first coaching opportunity in Cleveland, and to Brian, Tom, Ryan, Trip, Nails, Mike, Nemeth, Sean, Buddy, Doc Widow, John, and Bryan for sharing some or all of an incredible five year stretch in my rugby life. And thank you to all my St. Edward Eagle brothers that allowed me to work with them on their games. And of course, to my wife Courtney, for attending all the matches and events, interrupting her own life, watching me write at the kitchen table, and being a part of something I feel is special.

Many thanks for the support of the Cleveland Rovers and Cleveland Crusaders as this book has been launched, especially Ryan, Jason, Dale, Danny, Will, Mark, Dimes, Taryn & Kevin.

Outside of the rugby world, I owe much to authors like GM Lev Alburt, GM Roman Dzindzichashvili, and GM Eugene Perelshteyn, of "Chess Openings for White/Black, Explained" and my study thereof for the tone and approach of this book.

Contents

7

Introduction
- Purpose of the Book
- Description of the Diagrams

17

Elements of Attack
- Initiative
- Ball Speed
- Off-the-Ball Movement
- Communication

 Download a QR scanner on your smartphone to view all the videos throughout the book. Enjoy!

Tactics Using the Elements of Attack

SECTION 1
- **Exploiting Numerical Advantages**
- **The Pin**
- **The Scissor** – Two Versus One

SECTION 2
- **Attacking Defects in the Defense**
- **The Bounce** – Against Misaligned Defenses of Equal Number
- **The Crash** – Against Wide and Staggered Defenses of Equal Number
- **The Dummy Scissor** – Against Staggered Defenses of Equal Number
- **The Loop** – Against Wide and Staggered Defenses of Equal Number

SECTION 3
- **Combo Tactics That Create Defects in the Defense**
- **The Scissor Pin** – For Numerical Advantages with Tight Spacing
- **The Scissor Crash** – Against Even Numbers and a Flat Defense

Application of the Elements and Tactics to Structured Play

- **Reading the Defense** – Analytically Breaking Down a Defense
- **Example** – Applying Analytics to a Sample Situation
- **Attack Key** – A Primer for Applying the Correct Tactics
- **Attacking with Integrated Lines** – The Evolution of Option Attacks

Drills – Building Tactical Agility and Field Vision

- **Drill 1:** Establishing Extreme Changes in Direction that Matter.
- **Drill 2:** Establishing Field Vision and Complex Attacking, All in One.

Conclusion

Introduction   1

"I am thrilled to publish Break the Line, Second Edition. I've been lucky to benefit from the skills of London designer Simon Thompson, as well as the input from Phil Sharpe, Holt RFC head coach, on this new edition and to bring it to you.

Break the Line, in its Second Edition, is at the form I wanted it to be in 2017. It includes a new chapter with skill drills, commentary by Phil, and the benefit of QR codes, links to the techniques as used in the real world. The layout is attractive, diagrams are cleaner, and book more accessible than ever to the reader. I hope it has a lasting impact on its readership.

I am proud of the First Edition. It kept selling steadily throughout its four-year stretch, floating in the top 100 (and even, briefly, in the top 20) rugby books on Amazon. It has sold in the UK, France, Italy, Japan, Australia, and other places far from my hometown of Cleveland, Ohio. I've received feedback, both positive and negative. The book has endured.

As time passed and at my wife's urging, I thought about how to draft a second edition. I knew how much work the first edition took using a Word template and Photoshop for each diagram. It was hard. I could do it, but I needed some help to not just redesign the book, but recreate all the diagrams I meticulously crafted.

Finding Simon Thompson solved that problem for me, brilliantly devising a new layout, keeping the best aspects of the original book, and effortlessly handling the technical aspects of publishing. His creativity and experience in rugby publications helped immensely. I am glad to have him help present this book.

Then I thought to contact Phil Sharpe, a coach from the eastern shores of England, after he had left a positive comment on Amazon about the First Edition. He was interested in collaborating. After a couple Zoom calls across the Atlantic, I began to see that Phil was just the person necessary to bring life to the new book. He had a lifetime dedication to rugby, deep understanding of the game, and a shared interest in training young players and coaches how to approach it. His comments on the book are as insightful as they are valuable to getting a grasp on the very elemental rugby concepts found herein.

That said, thank you for reading the Second Edition; I hope you find it to be a useful tool in understanding the game we all love so much."

Rick

Introduction

 "I am excited to be involved in this project with Rick. I first saw his book a few years ago and was inspired by his thoughts and the clarity of his ideas. When Rick contacted me and we discussed our rugby and sporting backgrounds, it was clear that we would be able to collaborate positively on this book. I am hopeful that you, the reader, will benefit from the knowledge it took me years to gain.

When I first transitioned from playing to coaching, I wanted to source answers to my questions. I sought out books, mentors, players, and other coaches who I thought would supply me with a narrative of how to play. I realized soon after that what makes a good coach better is a methodology that encourages questions and not immediate answers. Coaching is an exploration. Within these pages I'm sure that you will get answers, but also more questions, all of which will help you find out who you are as a coach.

This book has been designed for the new player and coach, the more experienced, and everyone in between, with clearly set out ideas, beautifully illustrated diagrams, and instructive links to video footage.

I am positive that you will refer to this book again and again throughout your career. Hopefully, you will add your notes and be encouraged to share them. See this book as a tool that will help you to formulate your idea of attacking and breaking the line."

Phil

The Tackle Line
Breaking the Tackle Line prior to the Gain Line

▶ The object of this entire book is to focus players on breaking an imaginary line on the field: the "tackle" line. The tackle line is prior to the "gain" line, where the defense has positioned its players in an attempt to stop an offense. This book will start with the simplest advantages that allow a team to break the tackle line, and then analyze the more complex advantages that accomplish the same.

Gain Line

▶ Lateral line across the pitch, bisecting the ball, where the last breakdown or set piece occurred.

Tackle Line

▶ Line where the defense (triangles) physically encounters the offensive attack (circles), which is approximated here from a scrum:

▶ Without a focus on breaking the tackle line, an offensive backline makes a critical error. That same backline will typically run its attack to the gain line instead, and the tactics employed will not develop fast enough to be effective. The focus of every attack in rugby must necessarily be where the defense will be once the play develops. The focus cannot be where the defense was.

This type of anticipation allows the attackers to time their attack properly and have a realistic expectation of which tactics will work, and which will not. Thus, it is imperative for the backline to focus on first breaking the tackle line. They will breach the gain line in due time.

Introduction

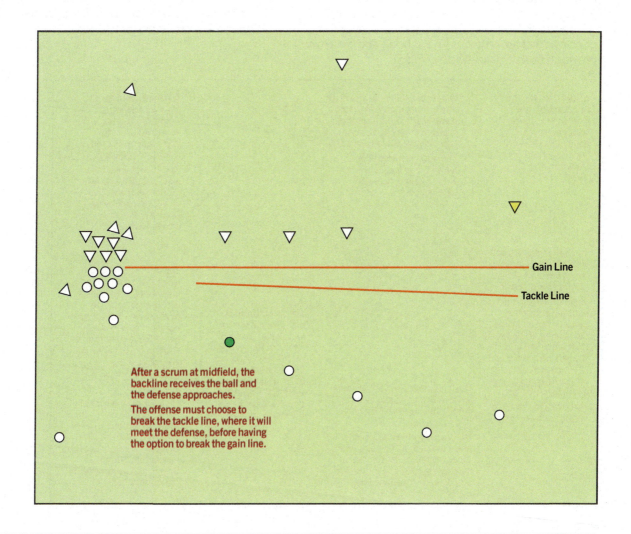

Break the Line – Analysis & Method

The Diagrams
Improving on the Status Quo

▶ Existing rugby diagrams, available online and in the manuals preceding this one, are not detailed enough. I decided to rethink the rugby diagram to convey the principles that are promoted in this book, and hopefully provide a fresh look at attacking rugby.

▶ Here is an example, miniaturized for this section only, which previews the detail that will be provided in the diagrams I've produced for this book:

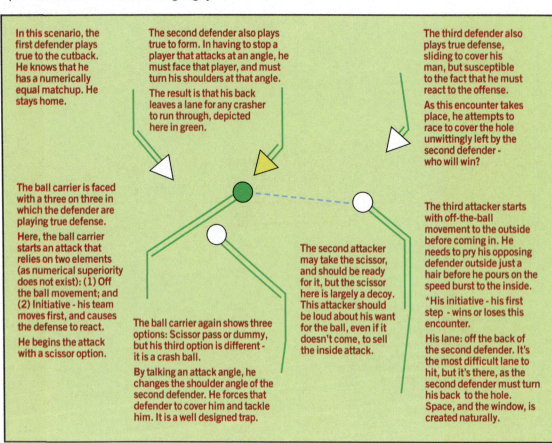

In this scenario, the first defender plays true to the cutback. He knows that he has a numerically equal matchup. He stays home.

The second defender also plays true to form. In having to stop a player that attacks at an angle, he must face that player, and must turn his shoulders at that angle.

The result is that his back leaves a lane for any crasher to run through, depicted here in green.

The third defender also plays true defense, sliding to cover his man, but susceptible to the fact that he must react to the offense.

As this encounter takes place, he attempts to race to cover the hole unwittingly left by the second defender - who will win?

The ball carrier is faced with a three on three in which the defender are playing true defense.

Here, the ball carrier starts an attack that relies on two elements (as numerical superiority does not exist): (1) Off the ball movement; and (2) Initiative - his team moves first, and causes the defense to react.

He begins the attack with a scissor option.

The ball carrier again shows three options: Scissor pass or dummy, but his third option is different - it is a crash ball.

By talking an attack angle, he changes the shoulder angle of the second defender. He forces that defender to cover him and tackle him. It is a well designed trap.

The second attacker may take the scissor, and should be ready for it, but the scissor here is largely a decoy. This attacker should be loud about his want for the ball, even if it doesn't come, to sell the inside attack.

The third attacker starts with off-the-ball movement to the outside before coming in. He needs to pry his opposing defender outside just a hair before he pours on the speed burst to the inside.

*His initiative - his first step - wins or loses this encounter.

His lane: off the back of the second defender. It's the most difficult lane to hit, but it's there, as the second defender must turn his back to the hole. Space, and the window, is created naturally.

Features of the Basic Diagrams

Offensive players:
▶ Circles, with the green circle being the ball carrier.

Defensive players:
▶ Triangles.

The lines:
▶ Where the runner has already ran.

Multiple Speeds (Single Line / Double Line):
▶ The single line in the diagram shows a standard speed and direction, running at 80-90%, while a double line shows 100% speed, known commonly as a "burst", taken typically at or around the tackle line, or to catch up with an attack at the tackle line.

Sharp Angles to Show Abrupt Changes in Direction:
▶ The angles are meant to be sharp, for reasons of offensive advantage, and typically the diagrams will show offensive players making off the ball movement of some kind. Take special care to note the angles of attack before the tackle line is met and before the offensive players hit their speed burst.

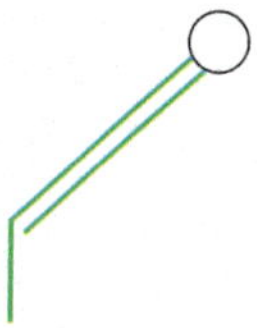

Defender Movement and Shoulder Angles:
▶ Each defender's speed and angle will be shown, as if an arrow. Their shoulder angle, diagrammed as the bottom of the triangle, is also shown. The "bottom" or flat part of the triangle is the back of the defender, while the point is his nose.

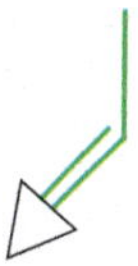

Passing Lines (Blue Dotted Lines):
▶ The blue dotted line can be either a potential or actual pass made during a given situation, to show either the option to pass or how the ball carrier received the ball. Finding the ball carrier, in green, shows you how he received the ball and how he might use it.

Focus of Attack (Yellow Defender):
▶ The yellow defender is the "target" of the attack. It is his defensive movement that is the most important, as one player is typically made the focus of the attack, be it a pin or a crash.

Features of the Enhanced Diagrams

▶ This book also provides a new form of enhanced diagram that will provide additional information on the technique involved. Here is a sample, miniaturized, that shows some of the depth in the diagrams, with the following features:

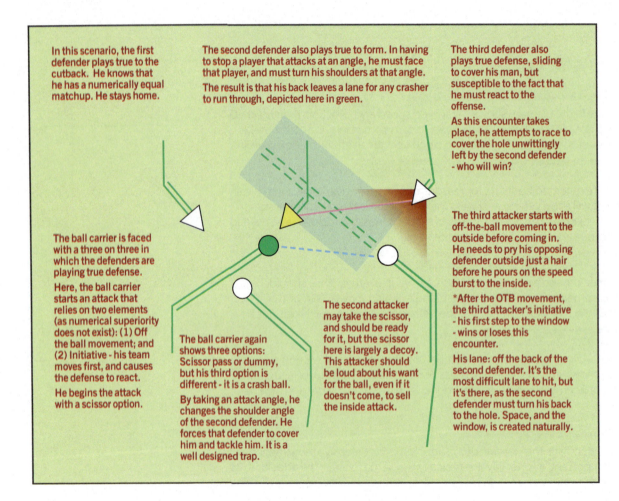

In this scenario, the first defender plays true to the cutback. He knows that he has a numerically equal matchup. He stays home.

The second defender also plays true to form. In having to stop a player that attacks at an angle, he must face that player, and must turn his shoulders at that angle.

The result is that his back leaves a lane for any crasher to run through, depicted here in green.

The third defender also plays true defense, sliding to cover his man, but susceptible to the fact that he must react to the offense.

As this encounter takes place, he attempts to race to cover the hole unwittingly left by the second defender - who will win?

The ball carrier is faced with a three on three in which the defenders are playing true defense.

Here, the ball carrier starts an attack that relies on two elements (as numerical superiority does not exist): (1) Off the ball movement; and (2) Initiative - his team moves first, and causes the defense to react.

He begins the attack with a scissor option.

The ball carrier again shows three options: Scissor pass or dummy, but his third option is different - it is a crash ball.

By taking an attack angle, he changes the shoulder angle of the second defender. He forces that defender to cover him and tackle him. It is a well designed trap.

The second attacker may take the scissor, and should be ready for it, but the scissor here is largely a decoy. This attacker should be loud about his want for the ball, even if it doesn't come, to sell the inside attack.

The third attacker starts with off-the-ball movement to the outside before coming in. He needs to pry his opposing defender outside just a hair before he pours on the speed burst to the inside.

*After the OTB movement, the third attacker's initiative - his first step to the window - wins or loses this encounter.

His lane: off the back of the second defender. It's the most difficult lane to hit, but it's there, as the second defender must turn his back to the hole. Space, and the window, is created naturally.

Introduction

Defender Strengths (Red Rays):

▶ Red emanating from a defender shows an area of tackling strength, while the absence of red shows the tackler's weakness.

Windows (Pink Line Between Key Defenders):

▶ Windows, depicted in pink, show the ideal plane through which a player should break the tackle line. You'll see why those windows are typically at an angle, not a flat line across the field.

Crashing Lanes (Green Rectangle):

▶ A green rectangle shows a safe crashing lane past the crashing window and behind a defender, a typical weakness in a defense, with the potential crashing line through that rectangle, shown as a dotted line.

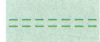

Time-Lapse Play Breakdowns:

▶ Where a play is complex, we will take our time looking at each step of the attack. Typically only one pass is shown (in light blue), and the action after the pass is not. This is because, if the diagrams are clear, the possibilities are obvious. Notes will clarify any ambiguities.

Notes provide extra commentary on each, diagrammed concept.

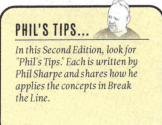

PHIL'S TIPS...

In this Second Edition, look for "Phil's Tips." Each is written by Phil Sharpe and shares how he applies the concepts in Break the Line.

Elements of Attack

The elements of attacking are the very basic principles that always apply to the offense in rugby. You should be able to share them with your teammates and students repeatedly, because they are indisputable truths. These elements are possessed by attacking players. They are distinct from the actions that must be taken, which will be covered in Chapter 2.

It is commonly known that players should attack space, use support players around them in an attack, and be active in supporting the ball carrier. Those players should also strive to score, which is the privilege of possession. Those directives, however, still beg questions about the manner of or reason for doing so. Only by exploring the questions behind those directives can an offense hone its effectiveness.

The advantages are identifiable as initiative, ball speed, off-the-ball movement, and communication. We will explore them in depth here.

Elements of Advantage

① <u>Initiative</u>
The Option to Direct Action

▶ The prime advantage of the offense is that it carries the ball and has the option to change the direction and speed of play, all without telling the defense. It is the option to act first, and thus force the defense to settle for reacting. The offense can exaggerate their advantage with drastic changes in the direction and speed of play.

Varying Speed

▶ One component of the offense's advantage is the ability to vary the speed of an attack. When this concept is applied to the ball carrier, it suggests that the ball carrier can gain an offensive advantage by altering his speed when he carries the ball. This is because running at a constant speed is more predictable, and thus defensible. Altering one's speed is a change that is less predictable.

Thus, an offensive player has much to gain from applying speed at the proper moment in time and space. This hidden "burst" of speed is meant to be applied before the defense can react in time to defend the change.

Varying Direction

▶ The other component of initiative is the ability of the offense to vary the direction of an attack at will. Applied to the ball carrier, it suggests an approach to the defender that maximizes the ball carrier's option to gain field position while limiting the defender's option to tackle.

An offensive player should endeavor to change direction towards open space, and force the defender to his side or back, to make a tackle more difficult and breaking the tackle line more likely. Changing direction quickly, and the angle of attack sharply, exaggerates this advantage to the defender's detriment.

A ball carrier demonstrates a successful change of speed and direction by achieving "lane separation," a term that will be relied on throughout this book. Lane separation is when any offensive player, with or without the ball, evades a defending player by leaving a tackle lane.

Elements of Attack

▶ The tackle lane is the prime tackling space forward of a defender. The ball carrier use initiative to leave that space, or lane, typically by means of an extreme change in both speed and direction:

PHIL'S TIPS...

"Accelerate towards the defence, check your pace to engage them, then change direction and accelerate simultaneously."

Inside Lane | **Tackle Lane** | **Outside Lane**

Think of the tackle lane as an area forward of the defender in which he can tackle without turning his shoulders prior to contact.

The ball carrier reaches a hypothetical inside lane (towards the center line of the pitch) by leaving the tackle lane before the defender has time to react.

Lane separation occurred here because the ball carrier (1) knew his plan and it was a secret to the defender; (2) exercised the option to change the direction and speed of the attack; and (3) took a radical change in speed and direction towards open space to do so, leaving the defender to his side.

Leave one of those elements out, and the ball carrier does not achieve the desired result.

▶ **LANE SEPARATION**
Goose stepping primes the runner to change speed and direction to create lane separation multiple times.

Break the Line – Analysis & Method

② Ball Speed
The Reason for Having Support that is Spaced and Available

▶ The ball, whether kicked or passed, travels faster than a defender can travel the same distance. An attacking team can utilize that to their advantage in numerous ways, by spacing themselves properly to allow the speed of the ball, when passed to create gains in field position.

The ball carrier thus need not do everything himself, but he must be able to pass accurately at a moment's notice, exploiting the areas where the defenders cannot cover. By holding the object of the game, the ball, with a special characteristic that it can exceed the running speed of any player on the field, the attacker has a distinct advantage.

③ Off-the-Ball Movement
The How and Why of Exacting Advantage Before a Support Player is the Ball Carrier

▶ Even if an attacker does not have the ball, the defense must react to him. He gets to do something that the defense has no luxury of doing - moving deceptively in relation to the position of the ball.

An attacker in support of the ball carrier has the option to show movement in one direction, while planning to attack in another direction. A crashing player, for instance, may simply drift to an outside lane, all the while planning to run a pattern to the inside. The defender is obligated to shadow that non-ball carrying attacker.

This slight advantage creates potential for the attacking team to manipulate a defender through deceptive movements, either to make a gap wider or to change the angle of a defender against the offense. In the end, the defender can be forced to move in ways that are to his disadvantage.

PHIL'S TIPS...

"The work rate of players off the ball is a key element to an attack and translates well to pressure the defence."

④ **Communication**
The Inherent Advantage of Creating an Imperfect Information Game for Your Opponent

▶ The offense has an advantage in communication. The simplest example is that a backline may call a play that is a secret to the defense. That called play is unknown to the defense.

This keeps the game one of near "perfect information" for the offense, like chess. At the same time, it make the game one of "imperfect information" for the defense, like poker.

In short, the offense can see the likely plan of the defense, but the defense is kept from learning the plan of the offense. This has obvious advantages when combined with initiative, because the defense is then made doubly unaware of how to react to the coordinated offensive attack. The defense is then less able to defend the offense.

But what of loose play, where no play is called?

The communications advantage still exists in open field play, given some pre-planning by the offense. For example, the attackers should all acknowledge a chain of command that starts with the ball carrier. Through the ball carrier's words, hand gestures, and movements, the offense can be directed in the attack. For example, as the ball carrier breaks at a thirty-five degree angle ten meters from the sideline, with a support player on the sideline, what is he communicating?

Most likely a "scissor" or "switch" attempt, which we will discuss fully later. If he makes the same movement in open space, that movement can be construed the same way, so long as the players are familiar with each other's body language and movements. A shout of "Scissor, scissor!" or shouting "Outside, outside!" will clarify discrepancies. Adding a pointing finger to where the ball carrier wants the support person to be will also help.

ELEMENTS OF ATTACK
A wide and quick attack shows the advantages of ball speed, communication, and off the ball positioning and movement.

▶ In the below diagram, explained later in the section on combination tactics, a break on an angle with a 3 on 2 offensive advantage communicates the attack to the support players instantly:

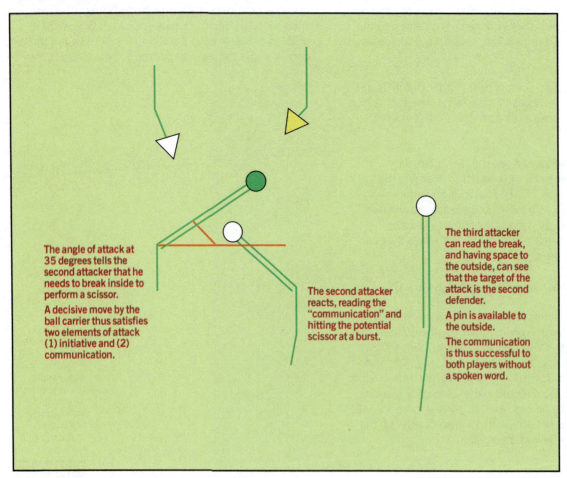

The angle of attack at 35 degrees tells the second attacker that he needs to break inside to perform a scissor.

A decisive move by the ball carrier thus satisfies two elements of attack (1) initiative and (2) communication.

The second attacker reacts, reading the "communication" and hitting the potential scissor at a burst.

The third attacker can read the break, and having space to the outside, can see that the target of the attack is the second defender.

A pin is available to the outside.

The communication is thus successful to both players without a spoken word.

Elements of Attack

▶ Even the ball carrier's straight approach to the tackle line can be construed as a "communication" if simply based on the realities that approaching a defense presents:

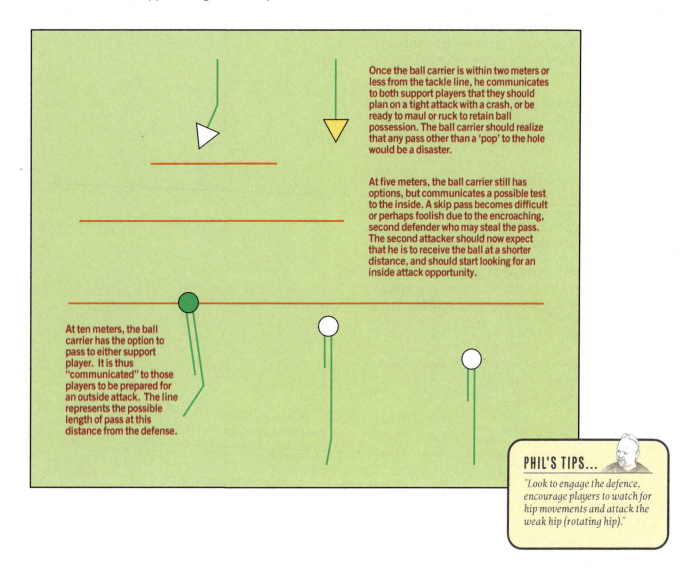

Once the ball carrier is within two meters or less from the tackle line, he communicates to both support players that they should plan on a tight attack with a crash, or be ready to maul or ruck to retain ball possession. The ball carrier should realize that any pass other than a 'pop' to the hole would be a disaster.

At five meters, the ball carrier still has options, but communicates a possible test to the inside. A skip pass becomes difficult or perhaps foolish due to the encroaching, second defender who may steal the pass. The second attacker should now expect that he is to receive the ball at a shorter distance, and should start looking for an inside attack opportunity.

At ten meters, the ball carrier has the option to pass to either support player. It is thus "communicated" to those players to be prepared for an outside attack. The line represents the possible length of pass at this distance from the defense.

PHIL'S TIPS...

"Look to engage the defence, encourage players to watch for hip movements and attack the weak hip (rotating hip)."

Break the Line – Analysis & Method

Elements of Attack

▶ In rugby, this sort of communication takes on special importance because there little to no stoppage of play, and the ball carrier needs to coordinate his supporting cast in order to be successful. If he is able to act first and also communicate instantaneously to his support, he exacts a significant advantage over the defense, even if the offense and defense are equal in athletic ability, fitness, strength, and skill.

▶ Applied together, these tactics become greater than the sum of their parts. They augment each other, make each other more powerful, and empower the players who use them.

When attacks fail, a player or coach can look back at the elements to analyze the source of the failure. Did the attackers sharply change angle and speed to space to create lane separation? Did the ball carrier pass the ball so slowly that the defender tracked in down? Were the attackers positioned so close together as to not take advantage of the field given to them? Did the support players not move off-the ball prior to the play, keeping their defensive counterpart in check?
All of these are valid questions relating to the use of the elements of attack.

These questions become more relevant when viewed in light of each tactic in Chapter 2.

Tactics Using the Elements of Attack

Each element can be applied to tactics, which then can become part of your strategy.

The focus of this chapter is on identifying and exploiting winnable situations. Once an advantage has been identified, the offense is expected to break the tackle line by exploiting that advantage. You as a coach or player should be thinking about your tactical advantages every time your team gains possession, at each set piece, and in each phase of play. In open field play, you should be able to identify the situation that reveals an advantage and act on it immediately.

But it starts here. An attacker first needs to be able to identify every tactical advantage.

That starts with the most common and best understood advantage, covered in section one, which is numbers. Literally, it is having a greater number of players in a given space than there are defenders. At its most basic, the advantage is two versus one. By exploring that simple advantage we can see how a numbers advantage can be exploited using the elements we know from Chapter 1. We can then draw some reliable conclusions about what it means to attack with three versus two, and four versus three.

The more nuanced advantage is covered in section two, whereby an offense encounters a defense that is misaligned, staggered, or wide. Even when the defense has equal numbers to the offense, it can be weak. These sorts of defects, in the way a defense approaches the tackle line, can be exploited by an observant offense given the proper tools.

And last, in section three we explore situations in which the offense creates advantage by applying combination tactics. Combination tactics can create defects in the defense, even when the defense is presenting equal numbers to the offense, or is playing the offense to its advantage. The offense, if mastering and applying all of the elements of attack, can make a losing situation into a winning situation, should it so choose.

The tactics that "win" those advantages are cataloged throughout this chapter, from the simplest to the most complex.

Capitalizing on Numerical Superiority

▶ The most common tactical maneuver in the game is to attack with numerical superiority. Typically two persons versus one, three versus two, or four versus three, and so on.

This is often called an "overload", but that term leaves a lot to be desired. I don't use it a lot here without further description, because it is vague by itself and often times conjures the image of an outside advantage. A numerical superiority, on the other hand, provides an advantage to the outside or inside. The key characteristic is the difference in numbers in a defined space.

Having a numerical advantage is significant because, except in rare instances, a defender cannot move to physically cover the space occupied by two attackers. There is no time for the defender to do so, and the laws of physics demand that his body be in one place at any given time. This is embodied by the element from Chapter 1 – the ball moves faster than any defender

Tactics based on numerical advantage should be the foundation of your open-field attacking philosophy. Such tactics pervade the entire game, and cannot be stressed enough. It seems rudimentary, but as you will see through the detail in this section, a backline can succeed merely by looking for numerical advantages - again, and again, and again.

The Pin
Against a Single Defender Pitted in the Lane Between Two Attackers

▶ Pinning is the attacker's answer to the most pure numerical advantage - two versus one. It occurs when one defender plays in a lane between two attackers, attempting to force an error by the ball carrier.

The attacking team maintains a distinct advantage on each pin. The ball carrier should force the defender to commit by taking a hard line to the inside, giving the ball carrier the opportunity to pass to the available support player, who then breaks the tackle line.

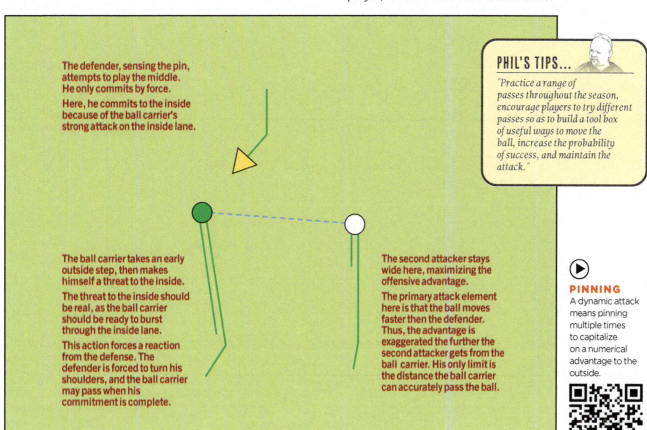

The defender, sensing the pin, attempts to play the middle. He only commits by force.

Here, he commits to the inside because of the ball carrier's strong attack on the inside lane.

The ball carrier takes an early outside step, then makes himself a threat to the inside.

The threat to the inside should be real, as the ball carrier should be ready to burst through the inside lane.

This action forces a reaction from the defense. The defender is forced to turn his shoulders, and the ball carrier may pass when his commitment is complete.

The second attacker stays wide here, maximizing the offensive advantage.

The primary attack element here is that the ball moves faster then the defender. Thus, the advantage is exaggerated the further the second attacker gets from the ball carrier. His only limit is the distance the ball carrier can accurately pass the ball.

PHIL'S TIPS...
"Practice a range of passes throughout the season, encourage players to try different passes so as to build a tool box of useful ways to move the ball, increase the probability of success, and maintain the attack."

PINNING
A dynamic attack means pinning multiple times to capitalize on a numerical advantage to the outside.

▶ The defender is forced away from the second attacker:

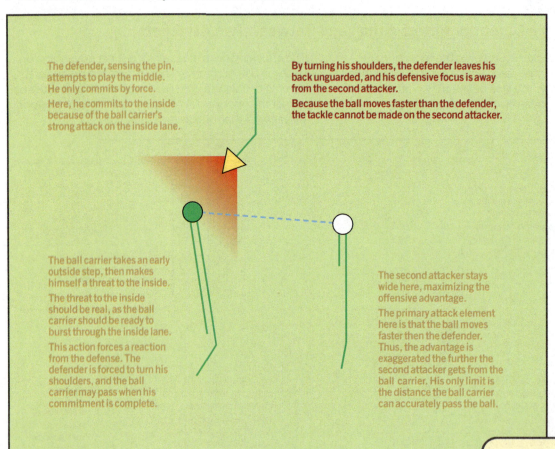

The defender, sensing the pin, attempts to play the middle. He only commits by force.

Here, he commits to the inside because of the ball carrier's strong attack on the inside lane.

By turning his shoulders, the defender leaves his back unguarded, and his defensive focus is away from the second attacker.

Because the ball moves faster than the defender, the tackle cannot be made on the second attacker.

The ball carrier takes an early outside step, then makes himself a threat to the inside.

The threat to the inside should be real, as the ball carrier should be ready to burst through the inside lane.

This action forces a reaction from the defense. The defender is forced to turn his shoulders, and the ball carrier may pass when his commitment is complete.

The second attacker stays wide here, maximizing the offensive advantage.

The primary attack element here is that the ball moves faster then the defender. Thus, the advantage is exaggerated the further the second attacker gets from the ball carrier. His only limit is the distance the ball carrier can accurately pass the ball.

Notes

Angles represent how and when a cut is made, and when a speed burst is applied by both attackers to ensure that the defender is reacting.

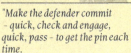

PHIL'S TIPS...
"*Make the defender commit - quick, check and engage, quick, pass - to get the pin each time.*"

Additional Notes - *Ruining Offensive Advantage with Spoilers:*

Spoiler – Drifting without Pace

▶ A true spoiler of a good pin is where the ball carrier runs, or "drifts", towards the outside lane and towards his own support player. In this situation, if there is no pressure from any other defender, it is a recipe for disaster. Why is this?

By drifting, the ball carrier gives up the advantage conferred by ball speed. The ball carrier forfeits the threat of an inside attack while simultaneously ceding ground to the outside; ground that otherwise could be covered by a pass in less time.

The advantage that is lost is the threat to the inside, and the distance the ball could travel that would outpace the defending man. If the ball carrier is not a threat to the inside, then there is no reason for the defender to stay near the inside lane, and no distance between him and the second attacker.

The result is typically that the ball carrier allows the defender to be in a physical space close to where both the ball carrier and the support player are. This increases the chances that the defender can physically address both attackers at once, because the attackers share the same space.

USING SPACING AND BALL SPEED TO PIN

Good spacing and passing signals the intent to use ball speed to win an encounter to the outside, pinning at the edge with pace.

Here, the attacker makes an error when he chooses to pin the defender, but takes no initiative against the defender, either in speed or direction change:

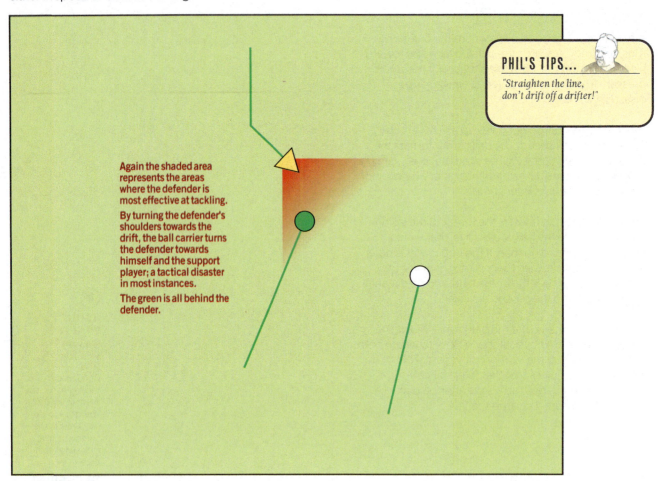

PHIL'S TIPS...
"Straighten the line, don't drift off a drifter!"

Again the shaded area represents the areas where the defender is most effective at tackling.

By turning the defender's shoulders towards the drift, the ball carrier turns the defender towards himself and the support player; a tactical disaster in most instances.

The green is all behind the defender.

Spoiler - Slow Movement by Ball Carrier

▶ The ball carrier can also spoil the action by his own malaise. If you slowly perform a tactic, you lose. All advantages in rugby are temporary.

As the ball carrier slows below his standard speed of 80-90%, his support slows, and the attack slows. By running too slow, there is no threat to the inside lane. The defender has a better chance to drift to the support player, successfully defending the play.

Spoiler - Soft Angles

▶ The ball carrier can also spoil a pin by taking soft angles to the inside, or not varying attack speed after the cut – forfeiting two of elements of a good attack.

The best example of this is where the ball carrier fails to make "lane separation" from the defender, meaning that he does not get to an open lane to run through and still has the defender directly in front of him. The ball carrier is thus not a threat to the inside lane.

The primary reason that this is a problem is that the defender will not be obligated to turn his shoulders, leaving the support man within his tackling range, as the diagram shows. The defender in this situation can just wait until the right moment and drift to the support man, covering a greater deal of space.

Scenarios

▶ Many players get discombobulated when additional attackers and defenders are added to the pinning scenario. This can be remedied. The key is to (1) understand which defender is the target of the attack, and (2) leave time for the pin on the target. The pin is still the goal.

This often time leaves a player with the conflicting goals of committing their defender and getting the ball out quickly. If the pass is made too soon, then the defenders can shift down to the next lane and compensate for the overload. If it is made too late, the ball is spoiled before it reaches the last attacker's hands, meaning, a tackle occurs before the pin can be made on the target defender.

The early movement of the ball carrier is thus key, and identical in purpose to the ball carrier in the two on one pin: force the defender's commitment to the inside lane, even if for a split second.

An offense should favor pinning when it has both greater numbers to the outside and ample space. While it is possible to win some situations through a scissor-pin, discussed later, it is oftentimes more efficient to pin the opposing players by relying more on ball speed and less player fitness to break the tackle line. Accordingly, in wide spaces, passing the ball down the line after noticing a numerical advantage is the most efficient attack.

In a three versus two scenario, the first movement and the spacing is nearly all that matters, setting the first defender to his lane, and leaving room to pin the final attacker:

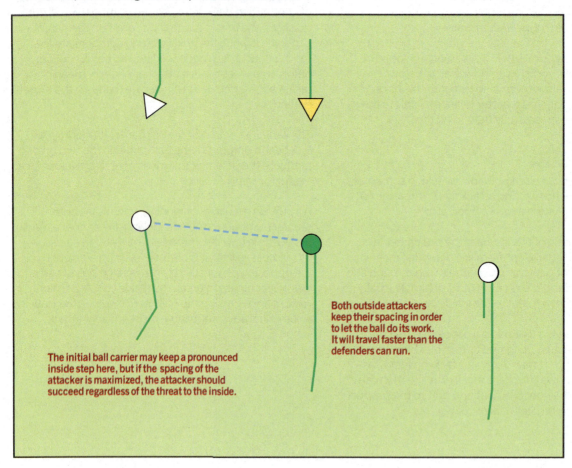

The initial ball carrier may keep a pronounced inside step here, but if the spacing of the attacker is maximized, the attacker should succeed regardless of the threat to the inside.

Both outside attackers keep their spacing in order to let the ball do its work. It will travel faster than the defenders can run.

▶ In a four versus three scenario, this can be done twice to isolate the third defender, who is then helpless to the pin. However, attackers should always favor the use of ball speed first. That means that if an outside overload exists, the attackers should prioritize passing, and make committing the defenders a secondary concern.

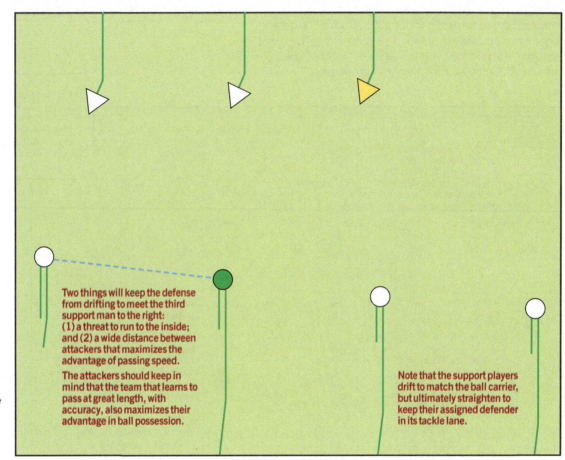

USING SPACING AND BALL SPEED TO PIN

Sending the ball early - favoring the pass immediately - gets the ball around the edge against a pressing defense.

Two things will keep the defense from drifting to meet the third support man to the right: (1) a threat to run to the inside; and (2) a wide distance between attackers that maximizes the advantage of passing speed.

The attackers should keep in mind that the team that learns to pass at great length, with accuracy, also maximizes their advantage in ball possession.

Note that the support players drift to match the ball carrier, but ultimately straighten to keep their assigned defender in its tackle lane.

Break the Line – Analysis & Method

Spoiler – Tight Offensive Alignments

▶ If the offense keeps a tight alignment and does not use all available space, the defense will have its best opportunity to "push" to the outside attackers to defend against an outside advantage. Put another way, by lining up tight, the offense limits the advantage of ball speed; that the ball moves faster than the defenders.

In the below example, the backline is tight and the pass is made early, so the defense has adjusted.

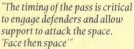

PHIL'S TIPS...

"The timing of the pass is critical to engage defenders and allow support to attack the space. 'Face then space'"

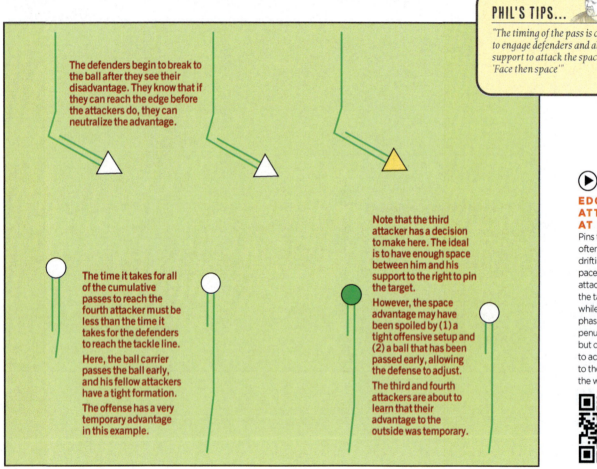

The defenders begin to break to the ball after they see their disadvantage. They know that if they can reach the edge before the attackers do, they can neutralize the advantage.

The time it takes for all of the cumulative passes to reach the fourth attacker must be less than the time it takes for the defenders to reach the tackle line.

Here, the ball carrier passes the ball early, and his fellow attackers have a tight formation.

The offense has a very temporary advantage in this example.

Note that the third attacker has a decision to make here. The ideal is to have enough space between him and his support to the right to pin the target.

However, the space advantage may have been spoiled by (1) a tight offensive setup and (2) a ball that has been passed early, allowing the defense to adjust.

The third and fourth attackers are about to learn that their advantage to the outside was temporary.

EDGE ATTACKING AT PACE

Pins to the outside often require some drifting, but at pace. A first phase attack breaks the tackle line, while the second phase fails at the penultimate pin, but only for failure to accurately pass to the outside for the win.

Spoiler – The Late Pass

▶ Even when a numerical advantage exists and the offense is properly spaced, the initial ball carrier can ruin an attack by holding the ball for too long.

This problem presents itself in structured play when a fly-half sees an outside overload in a four on three situation, but runs forward to commit the defense, only to have the defense meet his outside center to make a tackle before the advantage can be realized. It occurs in smaller pinning situations where the ball carrier simply does not trust his pass, holds the ball, and gets tackled.

Players must make a decision when it comes to both structured play and open field play – to pass outside or legitimately attack inside. The ball carrier cannot accomplish both attacks at the same time. Any step to the inside must be to set the defense only, and nothing more. Its overuse is ornamental and is a disservice to any attacking line, especially those that number in excess of two players.

Thus, a fly-half that sees a field-wide advantage off a lineout, scrum, ruck, or maul should favor passing immediately, even if it means doing so from a standstill position. The fly-half must know that there is a diminishing advantage to running towards the defense before passing the ball if doing so would sacrifice an outside overload.

The lineout leaves the largest cushion to run forward because it provides a minimum distance of twenty meters between the offensive backline and the defense, the position of the tackle line changes. Accordingly, a fly-half can run forward to create an inside threat and not immediately jeopardize his outside threat. He has time to do so because the defense is so far away. The more the fly-half runs forward, however, the less time is left to attack the outside.

When a scrum, ruck, or maul produces ball possession to the fly-half, there is little time or need to suggest an inside attack. The defense is already matched and does not need to be manipulated further. A fly-half running towards the tackle line in these instances actually diminishes the chance of pinning the outside, target defender.

In short, attackers must realize an outside advantage quickly by acting immediately, and that means favoring the pass to an inside threat.

The Scissor/Switch
Against a Single, Misaligned Defender

▶ The scissor, or switch, is the second method by which to win a two versus one. It capitalizes on poor defensive positioning and an extreme change in speed and direction by the ball carrier. The scissor allows the ball carrier to offload to a support player who crosses from the outside lane to the inside lane:

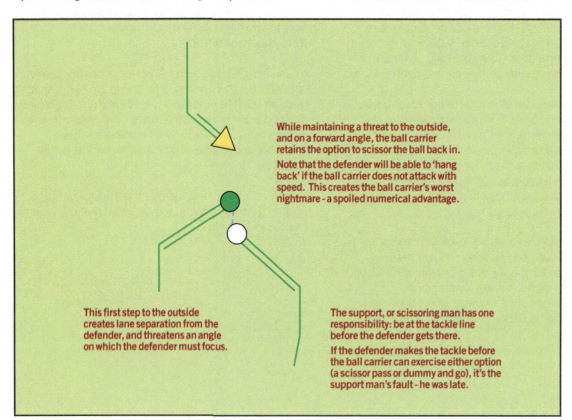

While maintaining a threat to the outside, and on a forward angle, the ball carrier retains the option to scissor the ball back in.

Note that the defender will be able to 'hang back' if the ball carrier does not attack with speed. This creates the ball carrier's worst nightmare - a spoiled numerical advantage.

This first step to the outside creates lane separation from the defender, and threatens an angle on which the defender must focus.

The support, or scissoring man has one responsibility: be at the tackle line before the defender gets there.

If the defender makes the tackle before the ball carrier can exercise either option (a scissor pass or dummy and go), it's the support man's fault - he was late.

Both players must be running at their burst well prior to the tackle line.

SCISSOR
Misaligned inside defenders are weak to the scissor.

The ball carrier takes an early cut at burst to either create lane separation or at least threaten a breakaway on the outside lane. The move forces commitment by the defender and forces the defender to pursue and turn his shoulders to the ball carrier. The ball carrier can then dump the ball off to the cutting support player.

This should be considered an "option" play for the ball carrier - he should be able to decide whether to pass or keep the ball and go, a "dummy" maneuver. The ball carrier, having two eyes, should keep one on the defender and one on his support player to ensure that the defender is tracking him and that an offload needs to occur. The ball carrier can then pop the ball at the proper time, or keep it and go.

Spoiler - The Ball Carrier Runs Backward

▶ The sure way to ruin a scissor attack is for the ball carrier to run backward to the support player. The ball carrier should always keep an "attack" angle, or forward facing posture towards the defense, even if just a few degrees' angle. The forward angle preserves the option of the ball carrier to, if the defender stays in the inside lane, run the ball to the outside lane after faking the pass. We will explore the fake or dummy pass more later as it applies to defensive weaknesses.

Spoiler - The Support Man is Late

• The support man should keep in mind that it is his responsibility - and solely his responsibility - to get to the tackle line in time before the ball carrier gets hit. Remember, the time that the support man possesses to get the tackle line is equal to, if not slightly less than, the time the defender will take to get to the ball carrier.

PHIL'S TIPS...

"When training for passing, you should include scissors to increase understanding of the spacing required to supporting running lines."

SCISSOR
Misaligned inside defenders are weak to the scissor.

SCISSOR
Trailing inside defenders leave the switch open.

Attacking Defects in the Defense

▶ If the game were only about counting how many players were on a particular area of the pitch, it probably would not be very exciting.

The reality is that good defenses minimize numerical disadvantages, and in many situations on the field completely eliminate them, such as in set plays near the goal line. All other numbers being equal then, the offense must find another way to use the elements of advantage to break the tackle line.

When numbers are equal, the offense must look for defects in the defensive line. Defects are by definition a weakness. In rugby, they can be defined as a defensive posture that decreases the defense's chance to tackle the ball carrier at the tackle line or otherwise prevent beneficial movement of the ball across the pitch.

Three common defects exist:

① **Alignment -**
One or more defensive tackle lanes are not lined up laterally over the attackers.

② **Width -**
Defensive tackle lanes are wider than the distance between two attackers, leaving inside space.

③ **Staggering -**
Defensive front is not "flat" at the tackle line, leaving angled windows of attack.

▶ While defenses are also weakened because of talent, skill level, or physical characteristics, those attributes will always be addressed in relation to the other three factors. After all, a defensive player who is limited in any one of those physical attributes can still properly align themselves, make proper spacing, and eliminate staggering.

Put another way, physical attributes of individual defense players are certainly relevant, but are most important and analyzable, for purposes of this book, *when those individual player attributes have caused or can cause some other defect in the defense.*

The Bounce
Against Misaligned Defenses

▶ A typical defensive weakness is a misalignment, whereby the defenders are not lined up over their offensive counterparts. This is a situation where lane separation has already occurred or can easily occur for the attacker.

The "bounce" is a maneuver to the outside that exploits this defensive weakness. It can be employed if the (1) the ball carrier has created lane separation to the outside of his assigned defender; (2) the offensive support player is fast enough to maintain near-equality with the ball carrier; and (3) the offensive support will not reach the sideline before the ball carrier reaches the tackle line (ie: the play won't run out of bounds before it is successful).

Alternately, a misalignment can be forced when a fleet-footed back encounters a flat-footed forward. That backline player may be able to create a misalignment by breaking hard to his opposing defender's outside, and can be successful if his cut is sharply angled and speed burst properly applied.

In either scenario, the bounce tactic actually changes the count of the matchup, artificially creating an outside overload and giving the offense an advantage even when the number of defenders was initially equal to the number of attackers.

▶ The bounce can create a pin opportunity to the outside:

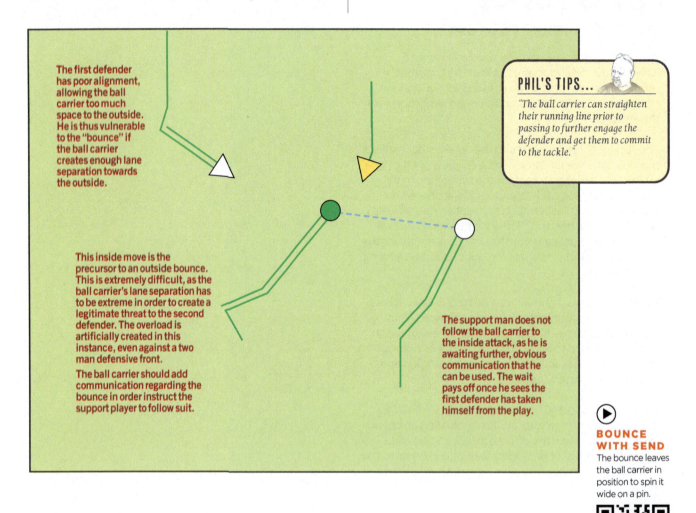

The first defender has poor alignment, allowing the ball carrier too much space to the outside. He is thus vulnerable to the "bounce" if the ball carrier creates enough lane separation towards the outside.

This inside move is the precursor to an outside bounce. This is extremely difficult, as the ball carrier's lane separation has to be extreme in order to create a legitimate threat to the second defender. The overload is artificially created in this instance, even against a two man defensive front.

The ball carrier should add communication regarding the bounce in order instruct the support player to follow suit.

The support man does not follow the ball carrier to the inside attack, as he is awaiting further, obvious communication that he can be used. The wait pays off once he sees the first defender has taken himself from the play.

PHIL'S TIPS...

"The ball carrier can straighten their running line prior to passing to further engage the defender and get them to commit to the tackle."

▶ **BOUNCE WITH SEND**
The bounce leaves the ball carrier in position to spin it wide on a pin.

▶ The bounce can also create a change in numerical superiority in a three on three situation:

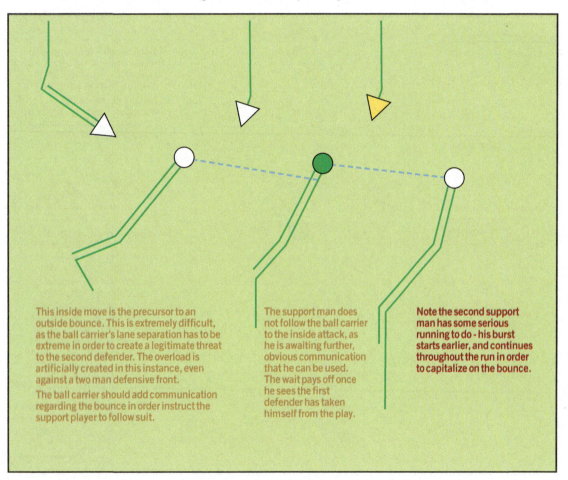

This inside move is the precursor to an outside bounce. This is extremely difficult, as the ball carrier's lane separation has to be extreme in order to create a legitimate threat to the second defender. The overload is artificially created in this instance, even against a two man defensive front.

The ball carrier should add communication regarding the bounce in order instruct the support player to follow suit.

The support man does not follow the ball carrier to the inside attack, as he is awaiting further, obvious communication that he can be used. The wait pays off once he sees the first defender has taken himself from the play.

Note the second support man has some serious running to do - his burst starts earlier, and continues throughout the run in order to capitalize on the bounce.

▶ This second example is possible but is the rarest, as it requires extreme athleticism from all support players that accompany the ball carrier. It starts with the ball carrier, though, who must have an athleticism that matches or exceeds his peers on both defense and offense.

▶ In either of the above examples, the situation can be won by the offense even if one of the sliding defensive players attempt to play soft (or even run backward) in an attempt to give the trailing defender time to catch the ball carrier.

As in the crash, shown later, the ball carrier simply needs to "ride the back" of the remaining defender, using the space behind him, shown here as a green rectangle:

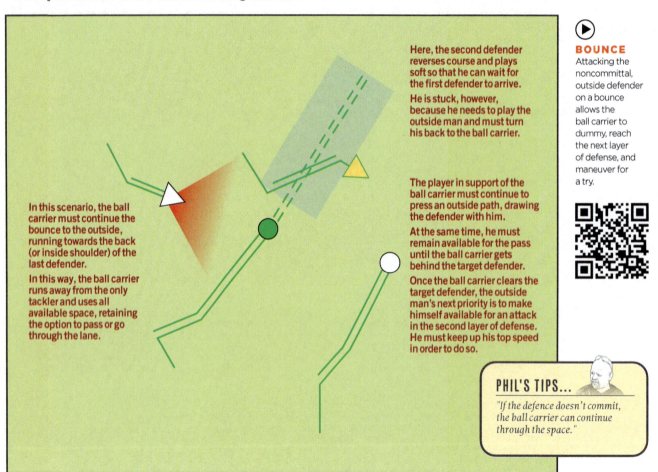

Here, the second defender reverses course and plays soft so that he can wait for the first defender to arrive.

He is stuck, however, because he needs to play the outside man and must turn his back to the ball carrier.

The player in support of the ball carrier must continue to press an outside path, drawing the defender with him.

At the same time, he must remain available for the pass until the ball carrier gets behind the target defender.

Once the ball carrier clears the target defender, the outside man's next priority is to make himself available for an attack in the second layer of defense. He must keep up his top speed in order to do so.

In this scenario, the ball carrier must continue the bounce to the outside, running towards the back (or inside shoulder) of the last defender.

In this way, the ball carrier runs away from the only tackler and uses all available space, retaining the option to pass or go through the lane.

BOUNCE
Attacking the noncommittal, outside defender on a bounce allows the ball carrier to dummy, reach the next layer of defense, and maneuver for a try.

PHIL'S TIPS...
"If the defence doesn't commit, the ball carrier can continue through the space."

The Crash

Against Wide and Staggered Defenses of Equal Number

▶ A crash is designed to break the tackle line when there are equal numbers of attackers and defenders.

There is no numerical advantage in a crash, so a crash might be considered an inside pin of sorts that must account for a second defender who has wide or staggered defensive alignment. Nonetheless, if executed properly, the crash takes an angle that cannot be defended by the late defender, and cannot be addressed by the target defender.

Setting the Crash

▶ On seeing a staggered defense, the ball carrier can set a crash by taking action to the inside lane, then straightening to attack. This draws the target defender inside and widens the crashing window. The ball carrier must straighten in order to create a legitimate threat to the target defender's inside shoulder and attack at full speed.

Window

▶ For a crash to truly work, the crashing player must understand that the concepts of the tackle line become skewed momentarily. If a defender is out of place, either staggered or wide, he will be late to his tackle. The line on which the late defender can make a tackle becomes angled, is not flat, and becomes a tool of the offense; it represents a "plane" or "window" through which the crashing player can run.

In order to succeed in a crash, the crashing player must be ready to cut directly into the angled window. In doing so, he creates additional distance between himself and the opposing defender. The crashing player should not worry that by evading his opposing defender, he gets closer to the target defender. He must trust that the ball carrier has sufficiently committed the target defender's shoulders and that the crashing lane is clear. After clearing the second defender, the crashing player can straighten up the field for his next attack.

▶ Crashing windows on the rugby pitch have three common characteristics (1) they are open temporarily; (2) they are not typically flat against the field; and (3) they are meant to be crashed through at full speed.

A crash is appropriate against staggered defenses of equal number:

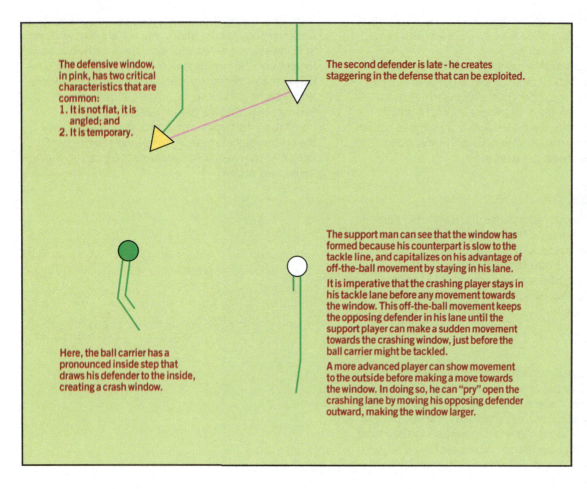

The defensive window, in pink, has two critical characteristics that are common:
1. It is not flat, it is angled; and
2. It is temporary.

The second defender is late - he creates staggering in the defense that can be exploited.

Here, the ball carrier has a pronounced inside step that draws his defender to the inside, creating a crash window.

The support man can see that the window has formed because his counterpart is slow to the tackle line, and capitalizes on his advantage of off-the-ball movement by staying in his lane.

It is imperative that the crashing player stays in his tackle lane before any movement towards the window. This off-the-ball movement keeps the opposing defender in his lane until the support player can make a sudden movement towards the crashing window, just before the ball carrier might be tackled.

A more advanced player can show movement to the outside before making a move towards the window. In doing so, he can "pry" open the crashing lane by moving his opposing defender outward, making the window larger.

CRASH
A misaligned outside defender makes a window for a crash.

CRASH ANGLE
Attack angle is everything in a well paced crash, allowing the attack to split the defense.

Tactics

▶ A crashing player must hit the window perpendicular to its plane. Doing so produces the most desirable result, as it is the furthest distance from his defender, is on the opposite side of the target defender, and leaves room to crash even further to the inside:

PHIL'S TIPS...

"Watching the defender's hips here will help the attacking player identify where and when the defender has rotated and opened a weak hip. Attack the weak shoulder."

As the play progresses and the first defender must track on the encroaching ball carrier, the window opens further - it gets wider.

The first defender is not only a distance from the second attacker, his shoulders are turned away - he has nobody covering his back.

By charging hard first to the inside, then straightening to meet the defender, the ball carrier creates a legitimate threat on the inside shoulder of the defender. This turns the defender's shoulders away from the crashing player.

The ball carrier has the advantage of seeing the approach of his support. The ball carrier pulls up once he sees commitment to pop off the ball to his crashing support player.

The crashing player capitalizes on his advantage of initiative by suddenly and sharply changing speed and direction towards the window.

Note that his angle is made relative to the window, not the tackle line. It is ok for him to be running a hard angle here until he breaks the window.

Also, note that the angle that the support man takes favors the inside, towards the back of the first defender. This is an important detail.

▶ **CRASHING WITH SPEED**
A wide outside defender leaves a gap for a crash at pace.

Break the Line – Analysis & Method **47**

▶ After the attacker breaks through the window, he must run up the field and maintain forward momentum. It will most certainly be the path of least resistance to the try zone and the location of the next layer of defense:

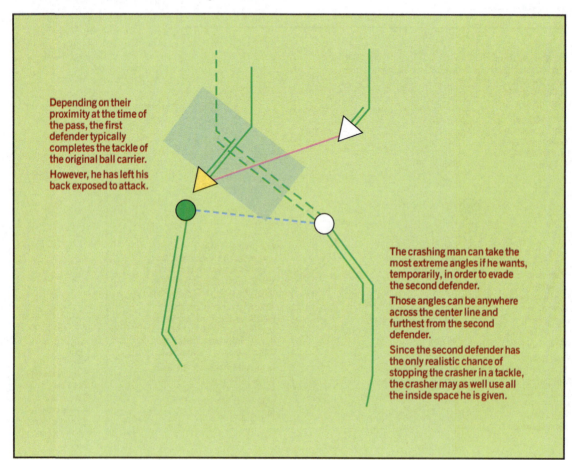

Depending on their proximity at the time of the pass, the first defender typically completes the tackle of the original ball carrier.

However, he has left his back exposed to attack.

The crashing man can take the most extreme angles if he wants, temporarily, in order to evade the second defender.

Those angles can be anywhere across the center line and furthest from the second defender.

Since the second defender has the only realistic chance of stopping the crasher in a tackle, the crasher may as well use all the inside space he is given.

HITTING THE WINDOW

By taking the proper angle with speed, a crashing player can slice through a sliding defense of greater numbers.

Tactics

Using the Space behind the Target Defender

▶ The reality that most crashers will find is that, if they look closely, there is an abundance of space behind the target defender on a crash, just as there was on the outside defender during the bounce.

Because the target defender does not have arms that are designed to make tackles behind his back, the crasher can theoretically run directly behind the back of the first defender until he clears the tackle line - "riding his back" until he can straighten up to the second layer of defense:

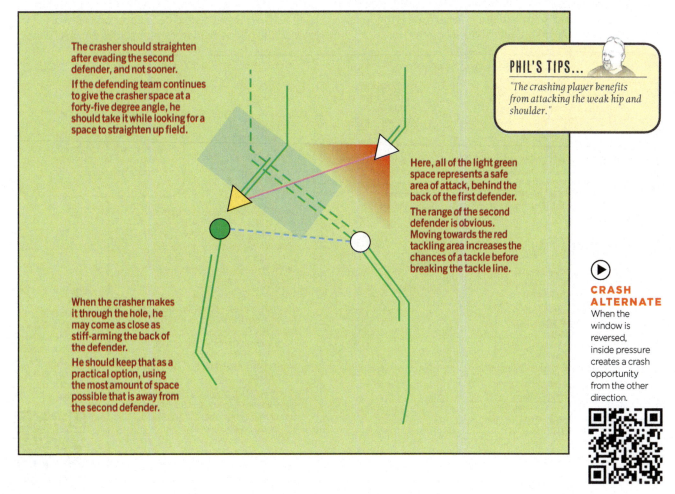

The crasher should straighten after evading the second defender, and not sooner.

If the defending team continues to give the crasher space at a forty-five degree angle, he should take it while looking for a space to straighten up field.

When the crasher makes it through the hole, he may come as close as stiff-arming the back of the defender.

He should keep that as a practical option, using the most amount of space possible that is away from the second defender.

Here, all of the light green space represents a safe area of attack, behind the back of the first defender.

The range of the second defender is obvious. Moving towards the red tackling area increases the chances of a tackle before breaking the tackle line.

PHIL'S TIPS...
"The crashing player benefits from attacking the weak hip and shoulder."

▶ **CRASH ALTERNATE**
When the window is reversed, inside pressure creates a crash opportunity from the other direction.

Break the Line – Analysis & Method

The Dummy Scissor
Against Staggered Defenses of Equal Number

▶ When the first defender is overzealous and attacks the outside lane too quickly, this changes the use of the scissor attack. The unevenness creates a different opportunity - allowing the ball carrier to exploit the tendencies of the defense during a scissor move.

▶ Here, the over-pursuit of an outside man creates an inside window to exploit. As the scissoring player and the ball carrier cross paths, the first defender (who is in position) is left with a Hobbesian choice to cover one of two lanes. If the offensive player keeps an eye on which lane

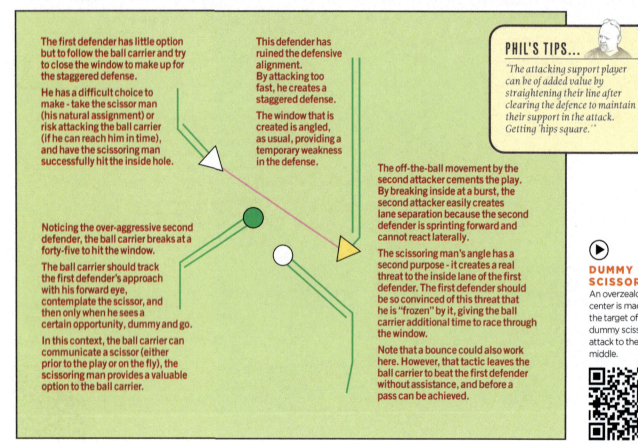

The first defender has little option but to follow the ball carrier and try to close the window to make up for the staggered defense.

He has a difficult choice to make - take the scissor man (his natural assignment) or risk attacking the ball carrier (if he can reach him in time), and have the scissoring man successfully hit the inside hole.

Noticing the over-aggressive second defender, the ball carrier breaks at a forty-five to hit the window.

The ball carrier should track the first defender's approach with his forward eye, contemplate the scissor, and then only when he sees a certain opportunity, dummy and go.

In this context, the ball carrier can communicate a scissor (either prior to the play or on the fly), the scissoring man provides a valuable option to the ball carrier.

This defender has ruined the defensive alignment. By attacking too fast, he creates a staggered defense.

The window that is created is angled, as usual, providing a temporary weakness in the defense.

The off-the-ball movement by the second attacker cements the play. By breaking inside at a burst, the second attacker easily creates lane separation because the second defender is sprinting forward and cannot react laterally.

The scissoring man's angle has a second purpose - it creates a real threat to the inside lane of the first defender. The first defender should be so convinced of this threat that he is "frozen" by it, giving the ball carrier additional time to race through the window.

Note that a bounce could also work here. However, that tactic leaves the ball carrier to beat the first defender without assistance, and before a pass can be achieved.

PHIL'S TIPS...

"The attacking support player can be of added value by straightening their line after clearing the defence to maintain their support in the attack. Getting 'hips square.'"

▶ **DUMMY SCISSOR**
An overzealous center is made the target of a dummy scissor attack to the middle.

the first defender commits to, he can either complete the scissor or effectuate the dummy through the window:

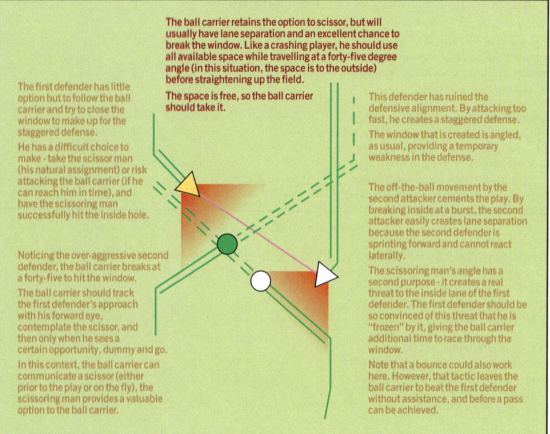

The first defender has little option but to follow the ball carrier and try to close the window to make up for the staggered defense.

He has a difficult choice to make - take the scissor man (his natural assignment) or risk attacking the ball carrier (if he can reach him in time), and have the scissoring man successfully hit the inside hole.

Noticing the over-aggressive second defender, the ball carrier breaks at a forty-five to hit the window.

The ball carrier should track the first defender's approach with his forward eye, contemplate the scissor, and then only when he sees a certain opportunity, dummy and go.

In this context, the ball carrier can communicate a scissor (either prior to the play or on the fly), the scissoring man provides a valuable option to the ball carrier.

The ball carrier retains the option to scissor, but will usually have lane separation and an excellent chance to break the window. Like a crashing player, he should use all available space while travelling at a forty-five degree angle (in this situation, the space is to the outside) before straightening up the field.

The space is free, so the ball carrier should take it.

This defender has ruined the defensive alignment. By attacking too fast, he creates a staggered defense.

The window that is created is angled, as usual, providing a temporary weakness in the defense.

The off-the-ball movement by the second attacker cements the play. By breaking inside at a burst, the second attacker easily creates lane separation because the second defender is sprinting forward and cannot react laterally.

The scissoring man's angle has a second purpose - it creates a real threat to the inside lane of the first defender. The first defender should be so convinced of this threat that he is "frozen" by it, giving the ball carrier additional time to race through the window.

Note that a bounce could also work here. However, that tactic leaves the ball carrier to beat the first defender without assistance, and before a pass can be achieved.

DUMMY SCISSOR
The wide, outside defender can be made flat footed while the inside defender is rendered useless by a dynamic dummy scissor.

DUMMY SCISSOR TO ATTACK
A dummy scissor baits two defenders and leaves a clear path for the ball carrier.

▶ Just as in a traditional crash, the dummying ball carrier can break the window, having the same option to attack space behind the second defender.

Once through the tackle line, the attacker has many possibilities, including an opening for an attack on the second layer of defense that can produce a score, a substantial change in field position, or momentum change. Either way, the dummy is a deadly attack on an uneven defense. A team's backline attack strategy, in fact, should deign to use this to break the tackle line on a consistent basis.

The Loop
Against Wide and Staggered Defenses of Equal Number

▶ Often construed as a way to produce an outside overload on a section of the defense, the loop best functions to capitalize on unevenness in the defensive line. It exerts pressure on the inside first.

The loop can be used to provide support to an attack, as in the second phase. However, it should not cause an outside overload because, as the ball carrier gives up the ball, the defender who previously covered him switches his assignment to the support man who received the pass, and a second defender slides to the outside. This is a common and necessary defensive adjustment.

Thus, the looping player's movement is entirely predictable to his new, defensive opponent. Since the new defender is outside of the looper, the looper cannot create lane separation to the outside because he is traveling to the inside of the new defender's lane. The defensive assignment has him covered.

What happens, however, is that the defense is sometimes tricked or habituated to over-pursue the supporting attackers on the outside, forgetting the looping man on the inside.

Tactics

▶ Defensive over-pursuit creates a window for the looping man to crash through along the way:

PHIL'S TIPS...

"This is very effective when used to focus the defence after a player that might previously crashed the ball up. Educate the defence to expect an attack and then change it. Practice this with all players."

Over pursuit by the second defender makes him the target of this attack, where a window has formed.

By virtue of his position on the field, the target defender either must double back to take the looping man, or have the looping man crash through the window.

The third defender is subject to being out of position, even in a scenario of even numbers.

Where there is an offensive numerical advantage, the defenders' over pursuit will create even more opportunities to pressure the inside first - from which outside pressure can be achieved.

The first attacker gives up control momentarily, but when he loops, he communicates his interest in an inside overload of the defense.

He should be prepared to receive the ball back almost immediately, from either side of the second attacker, before he sees the window.

After completing his loop, he may then either pass down the line, pin the target defender, or crash through the window.

The second attacker must angle his attack towards the first defender, as if on a crash.

The second attacker accomplishes two goals: (1) occupying the first defender at his widest inside position; and (2) making room for the looping man to speed through the hole created by the staggered (or space providing), second defender.

The third attacker's only serious option is to crash to the outside of the target defender and give the looping man an option.

Notes

The window in this example is at the same angle that is typically available in a bounce attack.

Break the Line – Analysis & Method 53

▶ The ball carrier faces pressure from the second defender immediately after making a movement to insert himself back into the line of attack, so he should change his speed and direction drastically towards the window. After receiving the ball, the looping ball carrier should break directly through the window:

PHIL'S TIPS...

"A good option here is to pass immediately. This is a good way to spread the attack from a set piece."

Over pursuit by the second defender makes him the target of this attack, where a window has formed.

By virtue of his position on the field, the target defender either must double back to take the looping man, or have the looping man crash through the window.

The third defender is subject to being out of position, even in a scenario of even numbers.

Where there is an offensive numerical advantage, the defenders' over pursuit will create even more opportunities to pressure the inside first - from which outside pressure can be achieved.

The first attacker gives up control momentarily, but when he loops, he communicates his interest in an inside overload of the defense.

He should be prepared to receive the ball back almost immediately, from either side of the second attacker, before he sees the window.

After completing his loop, he may then either pass down the line, pin the target defender, or crash through the window.

The second attacker must angle his attack towards the first defender, as if on a crash.

The second attacker accomplishes two goals: (1) occupying the first defender at his widest inside position; and (2) making room for the looping man to speed through the hole created by the staggered (or space providing), second defender.

The third attacker's only serious option is to crash to the outside of the target defender and give the looping man an option.

LOOP
This loop causes pressure on two defenders and closes the window, but leaves them vulnerable to the an outside attack.

▶ In this and all of the tactics in this chapter, the offense excels by using the elements of attack. Each of the movements in the loop require the offense, especially the looping man, to apply its mastery of initiative. The looping player changes the speed and direction of play throughout this tactic, and must do so in a way that is both extreme and not at all obvious to the defense.

The loop exemplifies the difficulty in mastering all of the elements from the first chapter, because the offense is forced to make so many deceptive movements through the tactic. It shows us that each change in speed and direction can mean the difference between being tackled and breaking the tackle line.

That is the larger theme in all attacking: Without dedication to fundamentals - the elements - the lines on the diagrams of the tactics are worthless. Communication must be established, off-the-ball positioning and movement must be precise, ball speed must be sharp, initiative must be seized, and changes in speed and direction must be extreme, or the tactics fail.

The third section of this chapter will show why this is true, as in that section, the defense will often be at no cognizable disadvantage in number or posture except to be subject to those very fundamental elements.

LOOP
Even a wide and late loop can lead to outside dummy pin attack.

Combo Tactics
Creating Defects in the Defense

▶ Now that we've observed each of the tactics that derive from the elements in Chapter 1, as well as the movements in sections one and two of this chapter, we can accept some additional truths:

① **The defense must react in predictable ways; *and***
② **A combination of tactics can be used to force that predictability.**

▶ It is useful to analogize chess to rugby for this section. The ideal game of attacking chess is one in which the attacker presents to their opponent choices, all of which are bad, that cause the opponent to gradually lose the game. Placing your opponent in a position of forced movement is called "zugzwang," translated from German is "compulsion to move." The larger, strategic victory in chess is comprised of smaller, tactical maneuvers that force good outcomes for the attacking player.

The game of strategic rugby are not much different than strategic chess. Rugby is about repeatedly creating an advantage with tactics that force good outcomes for one team, while forcing bad outcomes for the other team. Repetition of these tactics create a larger strategic advantage such as additional ball possession, meters gained, penalties, and points.

While there are no squares in rugby, the tactics in rugby can be analyzed like chess tactics. Like chess, rugby values the efficient use of time, space, power, and structure. The capabilities of each player can be distilled to a known quantity in space and time. Application of power is a necessary discipline in close quarters, while mastery of time and space, ball speed, and off-the-ball movement must be accomplished in open space.

The tactics in this section refer to these ideas. The tactics are drawn to give bad choices to your opponent, force movement, manipulate outcomes, and attempt to create a tactical advantage where the defense is seemingly even. They exploit largely the use of initiative, speed, and space to win.

The intent is to later work the combination tactics from open field play into a strategy that anticipates structured play, with set piece attacks, as we will discuss in chapter three. The combinations in this section become the basis for plays that are called after reading defensive alignments, and work directly into any offensive plan.

The Scissor Pin

For Numerical Advantages in Tight Spaces

▶ The scissor-pin is an excellent example of capitalizing on zugzwang, where the defense is forced to make a bad move and the offense retains all options to make a good move.

The scissor-pin is a combo movement that includes a scissor followed by a pin, and is applied to situations in which three attackers encounter two defenders, but passing down the line might be a bad idea. In tight space, attackers simply may not have the time to pass down the line and guarantee a win to the outside against a defense that either shifts quickly to the outside, or plays "soft" by backpedaling as far as possible and feigning tackles so as to draw a bad pass.

This substitute, combination attack should produce a significant offensive advantage, even in tighter spaces along the sidelines, because of the way the tactic forces bad defensive decisions. This tactic should be used whenever possible.

By this movement, the ball carrier creates four options: a possible scissor, dummy, pin, or bounce.

Each results in a win.

Option 1:

▶ When the first defender defends the scissoring player, and the second defender defends the ball carrier on the switch, it opens up the pin:

PHIL'S TIPS...

"Practice this using the 5m and 15m lines on the side of the pitch, reduce the width of the drill area to increase the pressure on the pass and develop skills."

The first defender has no choice here but to stay home and attempt a tackle in the inside lane.

He is made a non-factor by the scissor.

Note that the second defender has done his best at playing his position "soft" - he is playing an in-between lane position between the second and third attackers, and not sprinting to the tackle line.

Three on twos often fail because defenders notice and adjust to disadvantages in numbers in this exact way.

Nonetheless, with the offense deploying this tactic, the second defender is the target of the attack, and the victim of a pin.

The ball carrier is initially faced with a three on two in tight space to the outside - there is no option to send the ball down the line and take advantage of ball speed. Additionally, the defenders in this example, are playing soft.

The ball carrier, rather than leaving the encounter to chance, initiates a scissor to control the situation. He locks up the two defenders in the process.

At this juncture, the ball carrier has three options: Scissor pass, dummy, or pin the target.

The most common situation is shown here, where the second defender commits.

The pin is set here. The third attacker simply needs to be available on the outside.

DUMMY SCISSOR TO PIN

Even a weakly run scissor freezes the inside and allows the ball carrier to capitalize on an outside advantage in numbers.

Option 2:

▶ When the second defender takes the outside man, the ball carrier can keep on the dummy scissor:

PHIL'S TIPS...

"Any dummy move must be sold to the defence to be effective. Practice this with the outcome of believing that the pass will happen. Start by actually making the pass to ensure players know what it looks and feels like and then use this knowledge to make the dummy more believable."

The first defender again stays to the inside, but must give chase after the ball carrier crashes through the window.

His best hope is to try to track the ball carrier past the window.

This time, the second defender takes the outside man, leaving a crash window to the inside.

His hope can be that the first defender will not bite on the scissor, or will be fast enough to defend the scissoring man and then attempt to track the ball carrier.

The ball carrier is initially faced with a three on two in which the defenders, in this example, are playing soft.

The ball carrier, rather than leaving the play to chance, initiates a scissor to control the situation.

He can keep his eye almost entirely on the second defender to make his decision here.

At this juncture, the ball carrier is showing three options: Scissor pass, dummy, or pin the target.

Here, the second defender shows a play on the third defender. He leaves the center open for a dummy scissor and go.

The third attacker, in seeing that the ball carrier has taken the ball to the gap, still has an obligation to continue with the outside attack, draw the second defender outside, and continue his support of the attack.

DUMMY SCISSOR WITH SKIP

Proper body position, angled to attack, allows for double dummy that freezes the field, leading to an open outside advantage.

Option 3:

▶ When the first defender stays on the ball carrier, the ball carrier passes off to the scissoring support.

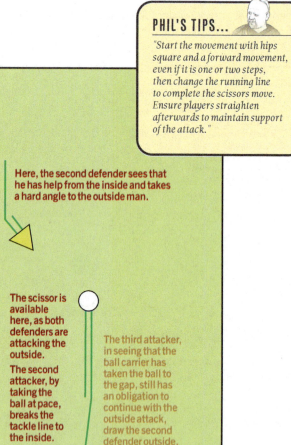

PHIL'S TIPS...

"Start the movement with hips square and a forward movement, even if it is one or two steps, then change the running line to complete the scissors move. Ensure players straighten afterwards to maintain support of the attack."

In this scenario, the first defender abandons his coverage on the scissor and takes a hard angle to attack the ball carrier quickly, either before or after the tackle line.

Here, the second defender sees that he has help from the inside and takes a hard angle to the outside man.

The ball carrier is initially faced with a three on two in which the defenders, in this example, are playing soft.

The ball carrier, rather than leaving the play to chance, initiates a scissor to control the situation.

He can keep his eye almost entirely on the second defender to make his decision here.

At this juncture, the ball carrier is showing three options: Scissor pass, dummy, or pin the target.

Here, the second defender shows a play on the third defender. He leaves the center open for a dummy scissor and go.

The scissor is available here, as both defenders are attacking the outside.

The second attacker, by taking the ball at pace, breaks the tackle line to the inside.

The third attacker, in seeing that the ball carrier has taken the ball to the gap, still has an obligation to continue with the outside attack, draw the second defender outside, and continue his support of the attack.

60

Option 4:

▶ When the first defender plays soft on the scissor, the ball carrier bounces to the outside defender, taking an aggressive angle behind the target defender.

PHIL'S TIPS...

"'Show and go'
Defenders will buy the dummy if it is sold well to them.

A double pump is often enough to check the defenders and then release if the attacker wants to sell a dummy and then make it real."

In this scenario, the first defender takes almost no option, plays "soft" on the scissor and attempts to shade the ball carrier to the hole.

He hopes to tackle the ball carrier despite the window, but must catch him first.

Here, the second defender sees that he has help from the inside, and takes a hard angle to the outside man.

This, as we know, exposes his back to the ball carrier, leaving space to run behind him.

The ball carrier is initially faced with a three on two in which the defenders, in this example, are playing soft.

The ball carrier, rather than leaving the play to chance, initiates a scissor to control the situation.

He can keep his eye almost entirely on the second defender to make his decision here.

At this juncture, the ball carrier is showing three options: Scissor pass, dummy, or pin the target.

Here, the second defender shows a play on the third defender. He leaves the center open for a dummy scissor and go.

The scissor is available here, but even if the dummy scissor has caused minimal hesitation in the first defender, the ball carrier has the opportunity to keep it and go.

The back of the target defender is exposed, leaving a lane for the ball carrier to run.

The ball carrier should take that angle until the pin is available, he scores, or until he has continuation from another source.

The third attacker, in seeing that the ball carrier has taken the ball to the gap, still has an obligation to continue with the outside attack, draw the second defender outside, and continue his support of the attack.

DUMMY SCISSOR TO ATTACK

A dummy scissor with a pin threat to the outside distracts the outside defender and gives the ball carrier ample running room to attack green space before straightening up field.

▶ You might say, why not just pass it down the line? There a numerous reasons. The first of which is that a three man attack in open field is a subject to extreme variability. Even the best ball carriers will spoil a three versus two opportunity by passing too quickly and allowing the defense to shift to the outside attackers. Another is that it is difficult for the ball carrier to perceive whether there is enough space to create an outside attack. The other is that passing down the line involves two passes, while the scissor-pin requires just one to break the tackle line – there is less of a chance for a knock on or errant pass attempt.

Primarily the scissor-pin should be the preferred method of attack because a ball carrier does not always have time to check the first defender and force him to the inside lane. The scissoring player forces this to happen for the attacking side. As we discussed on the section regarding the dummy move, the first defender is forced to make a Hobbesian choice to tackle the ball carrier or cover the inside lane, but cannot do both.

▶ Having acted first, and with burst, the attackers can establish the initiative before any of the lanes can be covered. The scissor man and the support player should both anticipate this maneuver once the numerical advantage is realized and once the ball carrier makes this first move. The communication, change in speed, change in direction, and ball flight should produce a winning result in every encounter.

Spoiler – Late Scissoring

▶ The unforced error that is typically made with this sure-fire combo tactic is a late attempt to scissor. First, a late scissor creates a flatter scissoring angle. This leaves the ball carrier with a less aggressive and more vulnerable line towards the defense. Some ball carriers go so far as to run backwards because the scissor attempt was so late. This is typically disastrous. Second, a late scissor attempt creates a flatter pass to the outside man, by necessity. This is a harder pass to make, and with a flatter attack angle, the defender can keep a hand in the passing lane and reach the pass. Third, a late scissor adds time pressure on the offense to either pass or go. All three effects need to be avoided.

PHIL'S TIPS...

"We want to educate the defence to make them predict and therefore predictable. Then we change. How many options can the players come up with in a training session from a single start point? When would they use them?"

The Scissor Crash
Against Even Numbers and a Flat Defense

▶ The scissor crash is not much different, but can be used when the offense and defense are equally matched - three attackers approach three defenders, one of the most difficult offensive approaches in rugby.
Because there are even numbers between the offense and the defense, three on each side in this example, the offense must act quickly and decisively to create advantage. This means sharp changes in speed and direction that create an opportunity for the offense in what otherwise looks like a stalemate. A disciplined backline should not feel lost here; it has weapons that exploit all of the above observations in the attacking game.

▶ In situations with equal numbers, all four elements must be emphasized to create a win:

① **Communication**
② **Off-the-Ball Positioning and Movement**
③ **Initiative**
④ **Ball Speed**

PHIL'S TIPS...
"Communication is a big topic, make sure players use specific communication to each other to build accuracy."

▶ Applying these elements puts the defense out of position to handle a well-timed attack, because each player understands the plan with prior communication, is properly aligned off the ball, changes both speed and direction in an extreme way, and is ready to dispense the ball quickly, even in tight space.

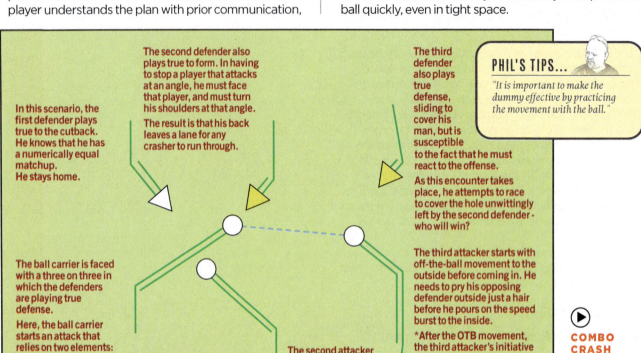

In this scenario, the first defender plays true to the cutback. He knows that he has a numerically equal matchup. He stays home.

The second defender also plays true to form. In having to stop a player that attacks at an angle, he must face that player, and must turn his shoulders at that angle.

The result is that his back leaves a lane for any crasher to run through.

The third defender also plays true defense, sliding to cover his man, but is susceptible to the fact that he must react to the offense.

As this encounter takes place, he attempts to race to cover the hole unwittingly left by the second defender - who will win?

The third attacker starts with off-the-ball movement to the outside before coming in. He needs to pry his opposing defender outside just a hair before he pours on the speed burst to the inside.

*After the OTB movement, the third attacker's initiative - his first step to the window - wins or loses this encounter.

His lane: off the back of the second defender. It's the most difficult lane to hit, but it's there, as the second defender must turn his back to the hole. Space, and the window, is created naturally.

The ball carrier is faced with a three on three in which the defenders are playing true defense.

Here, the ball carrier starts an attack that relies on two elements: (1) Off the ball movement; and (2) Initiative - his team moves first, and causes the defense to react.

He begins the attack with a scissor option.

The ball carrier again shows three options: Scissor pass or dummy, but his third option is different - it is a crash ball.

By taking an attack angle, he changes the shoulder angle of the second defender. He forces that defender to cover him and tackle him. It is a well designed trap.

The second attacker may take the scissor, and should be ready for it, but the scissor here is largely a decoy. This attacker should be loud about his want for the ball, even if it doesn't come, to sell the inside attack.

PHIL'S TIPS...

"It is important to make the dummy effective by practicing the movement with the ball."

COMBO CRASH

The combination of a scissor with an outside crash locks up inside defenders and allows an up-tempo attack on the tackle line with continuation for the try.

Tactics

▶ By virtue of the dummy scissor, the second defender must turn his shoulders to the support man on the outside. With some off the ball movement, the support player can become a crasher - he can ride the back of the second defender through the tackle line, running away from the third defender in the process:

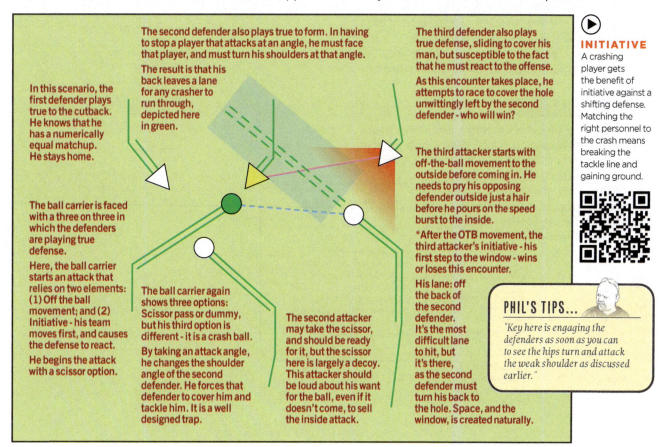

In this scenario, the first defender plays true to the cutback. He knows that he has a numerically equal matchup. He stays home.

The ball carrier is faced with a three on three in which the defenders are playing true defense.

Here, the ball carrier starts an attack that relies on two elements: (1) Off the ball movement; and (2) Initiative - his team moves first, and causes the defense to react.

He begins the attack with a scissor option.

The second defender also plays true to form. In having to stop a player that attacks at an angle, he must face that player, and must turn his shoulders at that angle.

The result is that his back leaves a lane for any crasher to run through, depicted here in green.

The ball carrier again shows three options: Scissor pass or dummy, but his third option is different - it is a crash ball. By taking an attack angle, he changes the shoulder angle of the second defender. He forces that defender to cover him and tackle him. It is a well designed trap.

The second attacker may take the scissor, and should be ready for it, but the scissor here is largely a decoy. This attacker should be loud about his want for the ball, even if it doesn't come, to sell the inside attack.

The third defender also plays true defense, sliding to cover his man, but susceptible to the fact that he must react to the offense.

As this encounter takes place, he attempts to race to cover the hole unwittingly left by the second defender - who will win?

The third attacker starts with off-the-ball movement to the outside before coming in. He needs to pry his opposing defender outside just a hair before he pours on the speed burst to the inside.

*After the OTB movement, the third attacker's initiative - his first step to the window - wins or loses this encounter.

His lane: off the back of the second defender. It's the most difficult lane to hit, but it's there, as the second defender must turn his back to the hole. Space, and the window, is created naturally.

▶ **INITIATIVE**
A crashing player gets the benefit of initiative against a shifting defense. Matching the right personnel to the crash means breaking the tackle line and gaining ground.

PHIL'S TIPS...
"Key here is engaging the defenders as soon as you can to see the hips turn and attack the weak shoulder as discussed earlier."

▶ The offensive win is possible because the third defender is forced to take an outside tack at the beginning of the sequence, and cannot track back fast enough to close the window.

The window is pried open further by virtue of the scissor attack. The second defender widens the window because he must turn his shoulders and step inside to cover the ball carrier. The second defender, having turned to cover his assignment, cannot react fast enough to turn and tackle the crashing player.

Break the Line – Analysis & Method

Tactics

Variation – Scissor & Bounce

▶ One variation can occur if the second defender plays tight to the first defender, sharing his lane. The ball carrier then could dummy scissor, separate from the second defender, and bounce to the outside. This would create an outside attack against the third defender, who then stands alone in defense. The pin should then be automatic.

Variation – Loop & Crash

▶ A variation can be run of this with a loop, rather than a scissor, at its beginning. A loop is also an acceptable, first movement in this attack. In the scissor crash, the ball carrier takes a hard angle and causes commitment by way of appreciable speed. This is not true for a loop, which often features softer attack angles and slower development.

VARIATION
Teams now dummy the crash itself - leaving support outside of this shape, doubling a feint to the inside and skipping to the outside with tremendous effect.

CONTINUATION
The double feint allows a team to attack at pace and recycle the ball for continuation. Here, the only failure is in failing to capitalize on the initiative gained after the crash.

PHIL'S TIPS...

"Train for as many scenarios as possible so when confronted with a defensive set up, the attack has a point of reference and tools to maintain the attack with confidence. Place defenders in different positions and start them from different places, change the drill zone to increase problem solving."

Applying Tactics to Structured Gameplay

4

All of the tactics in this book can be used in structured play, and all have been translated into plays used every day by clubs around the world.

The key for any team is to keep all of the stuff that makes their tactics work, but be able to run those tactics in from breakdowns and set pieces.

All tactics can and should be applied in the loose, but a great deal more success can come from tactics applied either after a stoppage in play or simply with a clean ball from a scrum-half. Each "clean" situation presents a special opportunity.

After all, an offense's communication advantage is at its highest when it can call a secret play against a predictable, attenuated defense.

But the reality is that players tend to become mechanical when running predesigned plays, losing all of the magic that makes open field attacking so dynamic. Why is that? Because players who run predesigned plays often focus on the form of the play, rather than the function of the attack.

In this chapter, we focus on running plays that maintain the attack first and worry about form later. We want each play to occur, but only if it has a specific purpose, exploiting a certain weakness in a defense, and only if it means using the elements of attack previously discussed in the book.

This means that as you apply this chapter, you apply the elements of attack to a particular target at the tackle line. Being specific about a target will focus the attackers on function instead of form. A predesigned play is nothing if it does not function as a specific attack.

To do so, look for the targets in this chapter. Note a target for each play you run. By being specific, you can make the structured attack a precarious moment for an opposing defense, not to mention an exciting opportunity for your offense.

▶ So here's a good breakdown of common plays and their translation to this book:

① **1-2 Crash -** *Crash between FH and IC*

② **1-3 Crash -** *Scissor Crash using FH, IC and OC*

③ **1-5 Crash -** *Scissor Crash using FH and FB, after a Dummy Scissors with the IC, OC, or both.*

④ **1-2 Scissor -** *Scissor between FH and pack, or FH and IC (depending on weakness).*

⑤ **1-3 Scissor -** *Dummy Scissor between the FH and IC followed by a Scissor between FH & OC.*

⑥ **1-2 Loop -** *Loop Crash between the FH and IC*

⑦ **Skip -** *Outside Attack which hopefully ends in a Crash by the OC and FB or a Pin for the FB and SSW*

▶ The next step in application is being able to choose which play to run, even with this very basic play set. When a defensive backline is set, what should compel one play to be called over the other?

The answer is: The play that employs the tactic that will create advantage, either in a line break or offensive continuity.

If there is no obvious defensive weakness, the answer is to create such a weakness by creating an expectation, then defying it. This considers the elements from an offense-wide, strategic viewpoint. After an expectation is built about the speed and direction of play, for example, the offense then can then run movements that counter that speed and direction to create a successful attack.

Reading the Defense

Breaking Down a Defense

▶ One of the most overwhelming problems a fly-half faces is seeing the field, or "reading the defense."

The fly-half must make command decisions on the field in order to apply tactics, but doing so can be difficult because there are so many people on the field at the same time. The fly-half simplifies this process for the ground attack by focusing on those players that can reach the tackle line and defend against his backline, and by counting those defenders against the number of attackers available to him:

Application

PHIL'S TIPS...

*"The players problem solving process can be assisted by his teammates feeding information in to him, by testing the defence and learning.
Use specific communication!"*

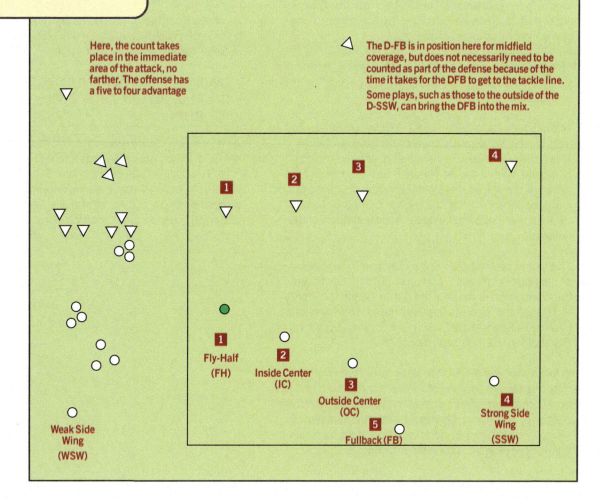

Here, the count takes place in the immediate area of the attack, no farther. The offense has a five to four advantage

The D-FB is in position here for midfield coverage, but does not necessarily need to be counted as part of the defense because of the time it takes for the DFB to get to the tackle line.

Some plays, such as those to the outside of the D-SSW, can bring the DFB into the mix.

1 Fly-Half (FH)
2 Inside Center (IC)
3 Outside Center (OC)
5 Fullback (FB)
4 Strong Side Wing (SSW)
Weak Side Wing (WSW)

Break the Line – Analysis & Method

▶ After examining those players in position to make a play on the tackle line, the fly-half can then "read" the field to guide how to attack using the tactics.

Three reads are necessary to do so: (1) A read of each individual defensive player's skills and abilities, (2) a read of the set position of the defense prior to touching or as touching the ball; and (3) remembering the historical actions of the defense in order to exploit them, taking into account numbers (1) and (2).

① Reading Your Opponent's Abilities – *Looking at them before whistle, during play, and for the whole match.*

▶ The read of individual athletes might include their height, weight, strength, speed, and tackling ability. This is the first and most common read of any coach or athlete. Who is the weak player on the other side? Where is the physical mismatch? Which opposing player is unseasoned in rugby, or a substitute for the starter? How can we exploit individuals to make defects in the defense?

This examination should not end at a pre-game peek of the opposing side's warm ups or films. It continues throughout the entirety of the game, during loose play by the ball carrier, and after the breakdown if possible. Examine who looks lost, who is afraid, who is tired. All of that looking will help inform a play call.

In loose play, the decision to dummy or scissor or pin may be made by looking at the eyes of the defender. His body position may tell you that the player is on the field, but the eyes will reveal he has lost interest in play, or that his body can no longer perform. The instant read might change the attacker's decision making.

This can and should be done by every player, even those supporting the ball carrier. In doing so, those players can read the defense themselves, make tactical decisions when they become the ball carrier, and report good reads back to the fly-half for use in the come plays: "The D-OC is slow," or "The SSW can't tackle me," or "The D-IC is huge, let's be sure to attack him at angles."

All of this information can be helpful if shared, even if some of it is disregarded. One thing is certain; it is useless if unobserved or kept secret.

② Reading the Set Position of the Defense – *Looking at them before they approach the tackle line.*

▶ A defense should be read based on its position on the field, which typically features the D-FB either set back in kick coverage or in the line. Because this book covers the ground attack exclusively, and does not discuss kicking tactics or strategies, we can simplify the common positions and considerations.

Application

While outside defensive overloads can exist, we'll keep things simple here and assume standard defense, with man-to-man matchups.

Near their own 22 meter mark and at midfield, the offense retains the advantage of a D-FB that is dropped back in kick coverage. Two variations mark the typical backline defense, the first of which is a wide D-SSW:

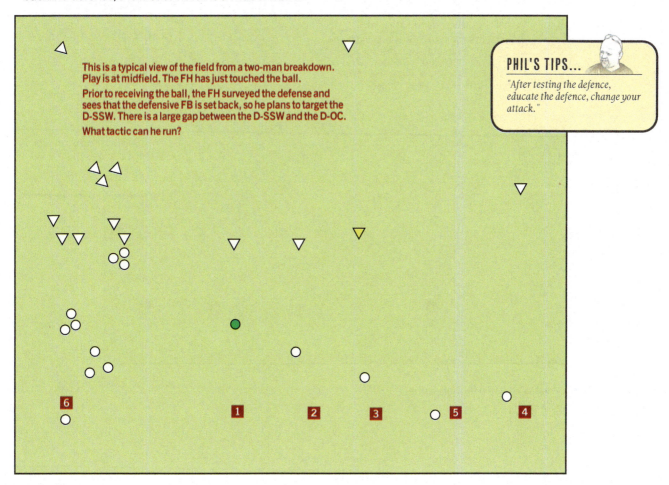

This is a typical view of the field from a two-man breakdown. Play is at midfield. The FH has just touched the ball.

Prior to receiving the ball, the FH surveyed the defense and sees that the defensive FB is set back, so he plans to target the D-SSW. There is a large gap between the D-SSW and the D-OC.

What tactic can he run?

PHIL'S TIPS...

"After testing the defence, educate the defence, change your attack."

Break the Line – Analysis & Method

▶ A second variation is the tight D-SSW:

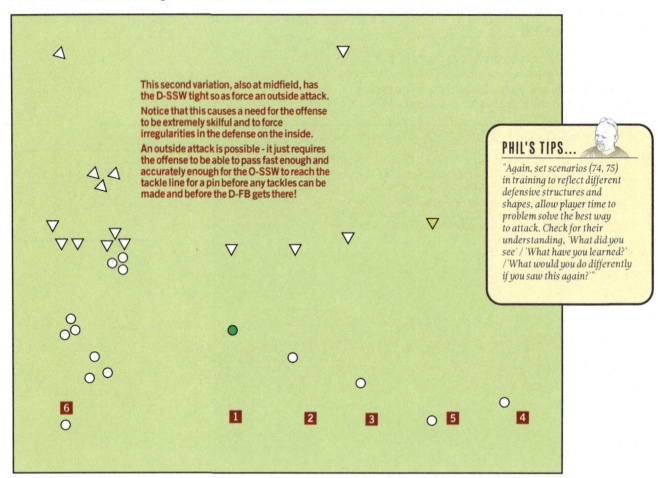

This second variation, also at midfield, has the D-SSW tight so as force an outside attack.

Notice that this causes a need for the offense to be extremely skilful and to force irregularities in the defense on the inside.

An outside attack is possible - it just requires the offense to be able to pass fast enough and accurately enough for the O-SSW to reach the tackle line for a pin before any tackles can be made and before the D-FB gets there!

PHIL'S TIPS...

"Again, set scenarios (74, 75) in training to reflect different defensive structures and shapes, allow player time to problem solve the best way to attack. Check for their understanding, 'What did you see' / 'What have you learned?' / 'What would you do differently if you saw this again?'"

▶ Reading either variation gives a fly-half some information to work with.

Application

▶ A closer examination might reveal other gaps such as a gap, with misalignment, at the centers:

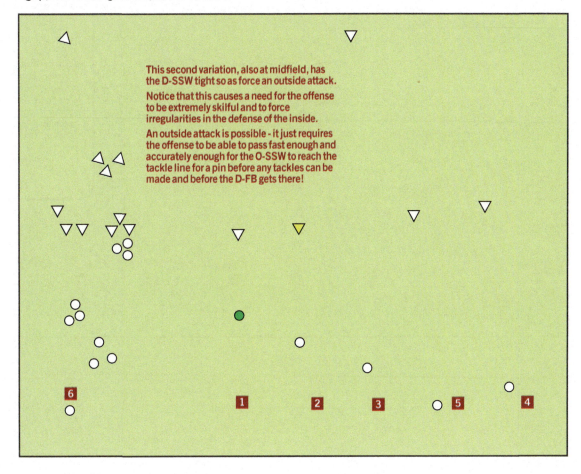

This second variation, also at midfield, has the D-SSW tight so as force an outside attack.

Notice that this causes a need for the offense to be extremely skilful and to force irregularities in the defense of the inside.

An outside attack is possible - it just requires the offense to be able to pass fast enough and accurately enough for the O-SSW to reach the tackle line for a pin before any tackles can be made and before the D-FB gets there!

Break the Line – Analysis & Method

▶ Or staggering at the centers:

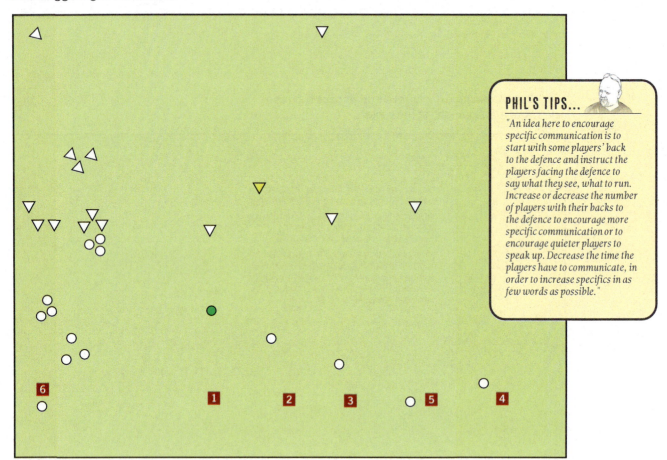

PHIL'S TIPS...

"An idea here to encourage specific communication is to start with some players' back to the defence and instruct the players facing the defence to say what they see, what to run. Increase or decrease the number of players with their backs to the defence to encourage more specific communication or to encourage quieter players to speak up. Decrease the time the players have to communicate, in order to increase specifics in as few words as possible."

▶ Or excess width between the D-FH and D-IC:

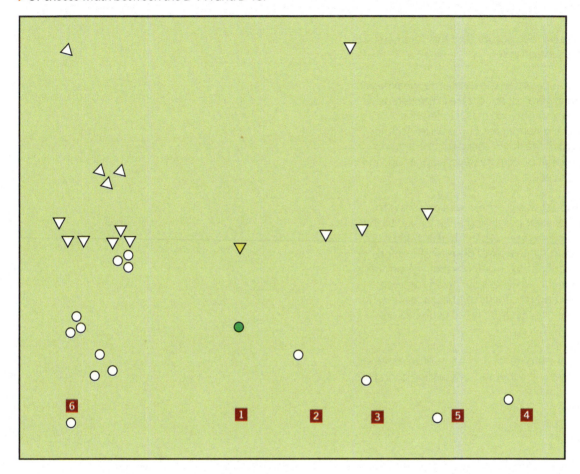

▶ All of this makes for useful information that can be applied to a play call.

All of it can also inform the movements of the attackers as the play unfolds, based on where the defender started from. One can expect, for example, a D-FB to have to run at full speed to make the tackle line. This can limit the D-FB to making a difficult tackle, at full speed, and without the ability to change direction. Knowing the D-FB starting position reveals that.

As this setup changes throughout the period of a match, a savvy attacker can then notice how much a defense is compensating for the weaknesses of its individual athletes. And in combination with the third read, can examine which plays are best to call in a given moment.

③ **Reading the Habits of the Defense –** *Examining the defensive approach to the tackle line.*

▶ The third defensive read occurs after the defense starts moving towards the offense.

As the defense approaches the tackle line, weakness may appear that were not noticeable in the defensive setup. Changes may also occur as the defense approaches. One defender might run wide. Another might approach too fast. Another might be lagging behind. These variations create gaps, staggering, and in general, opportunities.

One of the simplest ways to these weaknesses is to induce them. For example, calling several plays to the outside before calling several plays to the inside is a common method. Once a set of plays is attempted, they create reactions by the defense that will inevitably be repeated. Once a weakness during any analysis exists, it can be made the focus of a backline attack for an entire match, if necessary, if no adjustments are made by the defense.

But nearly every team shows some sort of weakness by one of their players, in some sort of situation during the game.

▶ A common weakness is the "cheating" center, looking for the big hit all game:

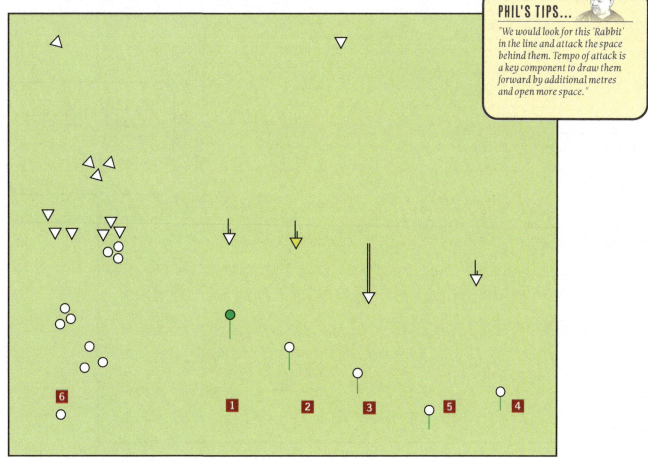

PHIL'S TIPS...

"We would look for this 'Rabbit' in the line and attack the space behind them. Tempo of attack is a key component to draw them forward by additional metres and open more space."

▶ This over-aggressive approach creates a "window" as we know. The defense is staggered, and therefore weak enough to run through. A dummy scissor attempt at that position, either by the FH or the IC, and with the OC, would tear the line to shreds, getting the offense to the second line of defense.

What would be left would be a D-FB, waiting to be victim to a pin between the breakaway player and his support, either the FB or SSW.

▶ Here's the window, just as we described it in prior chapters:

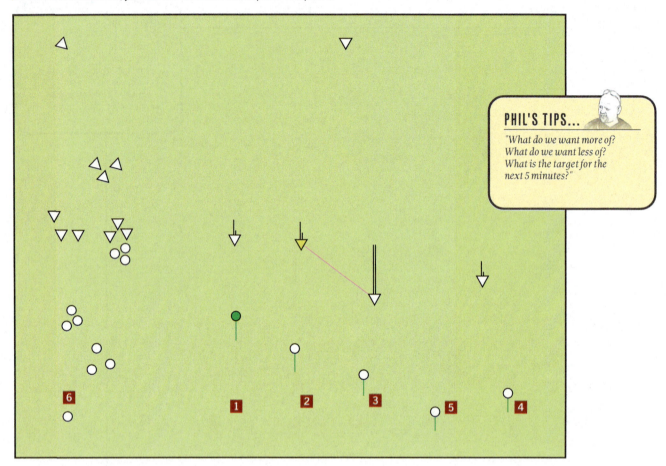

PHIL'S TIPS...
"What do we want more of? What do we want less of? What is the target for the next 5 minutes?"

▶ A dummy scissor by the IC, if not the FH (after dummying with the IC), crashes directly through it. Seeing that a D-OC does this on a regular basis gives a FH good information to act on.

▶ This "aggressive" move can be made by the D-OC, the D-IC, or the D-FH, all creating different weaknesses for a defense. Look at what happens when the D-IC is foolish enough to do it to a watchful offense:

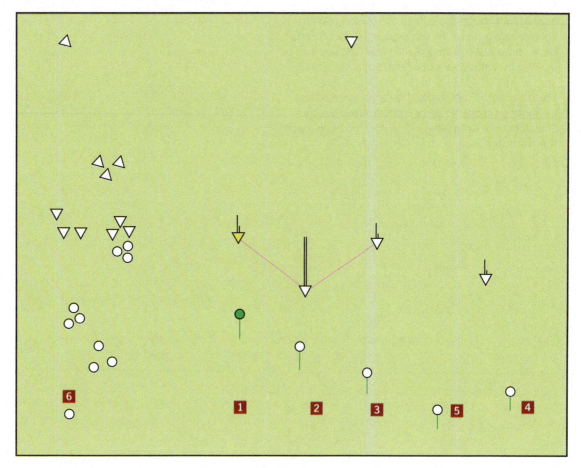

▶ Here, the D-IC is the weakness, and two windows open for the offense to exploit. The defense's position is unrecoverable if the FH is prescient enough to run a dummy scissor with the IC. Even if the ball is cast beyond the D-IC on a skip pass, the defense even shows weakness back towards the inside. The D-OC is forced to play both to the inside and outside of his tackle lane, leaving him vulnerable.

These tendencies should be examined and re-evaluated through the course of a match. Halftime is an excellent time to discuss tendencies, but this can be accomplished during play as well. The key is to be looking for what your opponent is or is not doing.

The defense will inevitably show you its weakness – it cannot be hidden. Perhaps discovering it at the final minute of the match will be enough to give your team an edge.

Reading the Defense
A First Example

▶ Imagine a match is in its fiftieth minute and your team has been making the three reads. You may use any of the tactics in this book to attack the defensive line, because your coach wants to keep the ball in hand.

Read type 1 – the defensive outside center is slower than the offensive outside center by several steps, even though he's an effective tackler.

Read type 2 – the line sets up tight at the centers, so as to stop inside attacks. The D-SSW sets up wide at midfield, moves to the inside to cover the gap, and allows the FB to fill to the outside.

Read type 3 – the defenders come up even, without deviating from the lanes they started in.

The situation typically develops like this:

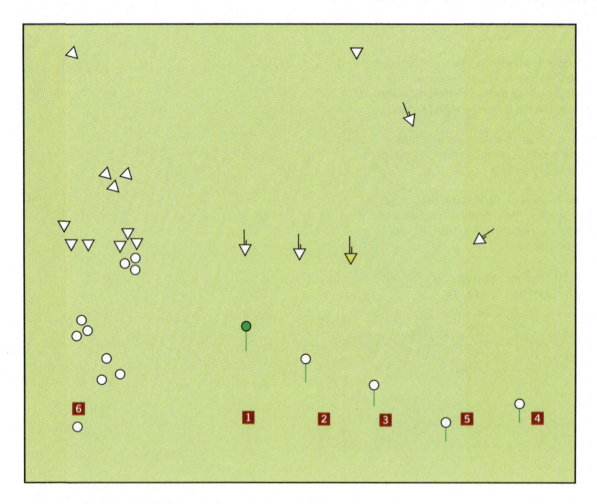

▶ Notice that our target is the outside center, the slow defender. Although subtle, he and the D-IC are set so tight that the offensive OC starts with lane separation to the outside.

So, perhaps with this information, a "bounce" by the IC and OC would be in order to get past the tackle line before the D-SSW can get to his position. Let's take a look how it would diagram out:

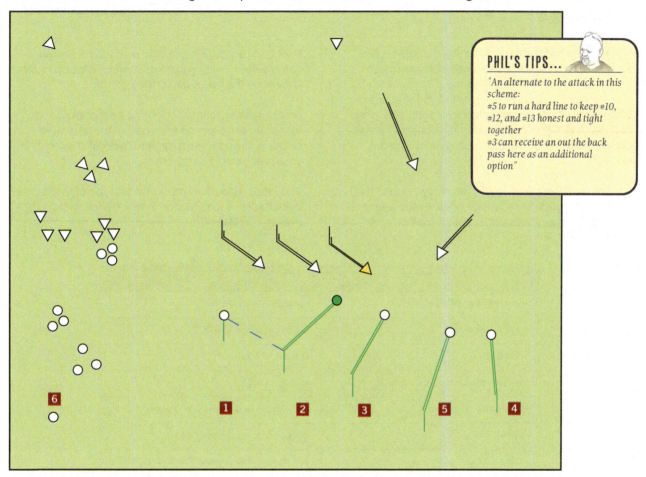

PHIL'S TIPS...

"An alternate to the attack in this scheme:
#5 to run a hard line to keep #10, #12, and #13 honest and tight together
#3 can receive an out the back pass here as an additional option"

▶ With a speed burst, the OC is testing the gap created between the D-OC and the D-SSW. The IC just needs to keep the pace up and provide a pass at the moment the OC is ready. Your OC, whom we have determined to be faster than the OC, has a better chance than not to hit this hole at full speed and break the tackle line. Does he score? It's certainly possible, with the D-FB forced to cover to the outside. The OC has created lane separation, and now simply needs to take advantage of it.

Break the Line – Analysis & Method

Preparation

An Attack Key

▶ This method can be used endlessly, to create endless assumptions with which to operate during a match.

The method begins prior to a game, looking at video of the opposing team and searching for defects in the defense. A player or coach can watch for weaknesses during the game, and adjust strategy as the match goes on.

A team, as a practice, should then study video of their own team to understand which weaknesses were not exploited, and which opportunities were lost.

Failing to review video of your own team's mistakes can create serious problems, whereby a team does not know why the fail, and why they succeed.

After a while, a team will develop a set of plays that exploit weaknesses on each part of the defensive backline, giving them a method to break the tackle line when each opportunity arises.

This key is a good example of what type of tactics may be helpful in each situation in which a full backline is available to attack:

Weakness	Play
• Over aggressive D-IC	• Dummy Scissor (FH & IC)
• Over aggressive D-OC	• Dummy Scissor (IC & OC)
• Late D-IC	• Crash (FH & IC)
• Late or Early-Sliding/Pushing D-OC	• Crash (FH & OC)
• Non-switching defender	• Scissor to that defender's original lane
• Wide FH & IC	• Crash / Dummy Scissor (FH & IC)
• Wide IC & OC	• Crash / Dummy Scissor (FH or IC w/ OC)
• Wide SSW that does not fill	• Crash (FH or OC w/ FB)
• SSW that does fill	• Pin to outside

Application

▶ Obviously, each tactic can be applied to other situations as well. Set pieces bring with them predictable, and thus favorable opportunities to apply tactics. Have a side of the scrum with a three on two advantage? Why not take it? By applying the tactics in this book to each scenario, you can be assured that you are pressuring the right part of the defense at the right time, and with the right tools.

Once a comprehensive kicking philosophy is applied to a rugby ground game, a team can then have a dual-threat attack plan. A team that is not breaking through in the ground game, but is still applying significant pressure on the ground, can leverage that pressure to improve their kicking game, and vice-versa. Well-placed tactical kicking only makes a ground game more formidable, as the defense attempts to cover all of the attacking methods applied by the offense.

PHIL'S TIPS...
"'Practice, Practice, Practice'
Practice until you don't get it wrong rather than until you get it right!"

Application

Attacking with Integrated Backlines
Complex Option Play with Backs and Forwards

▶ An evolution of the above attacking shapes has been to run an offensive line relatively flat to the defense using backs and forwards, anticipating ball possession and multiple phases of play to win an advantage. In this form, a team repeats a consistent attacking shape that presents several options to distribute the ball.

These attacking shapes use the principals discussed in the Second Edition, but with outlets for continuation. An entire, Third Edition could be written about how they should be deployed and may have to be written in the future.

The shapes are a necessity against crowded defensive fronts found in international play. A ball carrier must have several options to choose from based on an instant read of the field, conducted in the midst of play, and at pace.

A multitude of such plays are possible. Many have been charted online and within clubs, with results ranging from effective to incredible. It just takes imagination to tweak each and every one of the concepts found in the Second Edition, add attackers, and make new plays that have a positive impact for the offense. A quick Internet search of international highlights proves that experimentation can produce some incredible results.

You'll find that regardless of how those plays are made, or how the backline is set to the line, or what type of movements are designed into the attack, attacking players must focus on breaking the tackle line first, and do so using initiative, speed, change of direction, off the ball movement, and communication. Each of these elements is present in a successful attack.

The question for a coach or player will always be how to consistently and repeatedly produce a quality attack within the laws of the game that uses a range of player skill sets. The examples below provide a hint at the answer.

OPTIONS TO ATTACK
Layered attacking in a flat backline means options. Spot the first dummy crash, followed by a crash that seals the defense. A subsequent bounce on the weak side, followed by a clever inside pass, wins it.

CONTINUATION
Consistent application of an integrated attack produces continuation - phases upon phases from which an offense can break the line, even if a little at a time, and ultimately produce a try.

PRESSURE
Forwards are mixed in with backs to feint and crash inside in phases. In the second phase, numbers create a breakaway. In the third phase, layered attacking threatens the inside before it creates a win on the outside.

Photo by Quino Al

Drills – Building Tactical Agility & Field Vision

5

Each offensive skill that you develop in rugby typically deals with the basic technique necessary to accomplish the goal of the attack – catching, passing, scissoring, and bursting. Drills to learn these skills do not necessarily vary across clubs. In fact, you may come across the same drills in different clubs across the world.

What matters is the detail in the drill. In this section, we will discuss how to tease out more advanced attacking skills by modifying basic drills – particularly the "gauntlet" drill and the 2 v. 1 drill - in a way that enhances the impact of each of the elements taught in this book.

Photo by Max Leveridge

What was not discussed in the first edition of Break the Line is that the key to unlocking a player's potential is drilling the elements precisely and frequently until the point of mastery. This particularly includes the ability to be an off-the-ball player who can cut immediately and sharply when needed; a skill developed in a modified gauntlet drill.

The other aspect of a player's game that absolutely needs to be drilled is the ability to see the situations that could lead to success, and then execute on those situations. I would tell my players, "You should be able to win every single two on one advantage you ever encounter, all the time."

It also became mantra that a defect in the defense, even without numerical superiority, should be exploitable. Meaning, the attackers should win.

These drills help achieve those goals.

How often do you drill them? Every practice if possible, and particularly on "skill" days. Looking at old schedules I developed, I would incorporate gauntlet into the beginning of every practice for all players, and the modified 2 v. 1 / 2 v. 2 drill in each backline "breakout" session where possible. Even late in a season, a player benefits from refining their attacking posture, moving more precisely, taking correct angles, and conceptualizing complex situations.

Drill 1:
Establishing Extreme Changes in Direction that Matter

▶ During practice, the second offensive player in any attack is usually the subject of too little attention. That should change.

In applying the attacks in this book, you can see that the second attacker must always make sharp, off the ball movement. They must approach the tackle line at full speed, at an angle, near contact, catch the ball, and evade their defender. This is critical to breaking the tackle line for the offensive group.

In doing so, the player needs to change direction quickly, without unnecessary stutter steps. The change in direction, coupled with a speed burst at just the right moment in time, separates that player from the opposing defender's lane. This accomplishes both a measure of deception and evasion because the movement is not seen till the last moment by the defender.

Changing direction requires a serious measure of skill and attention to the ball. The ball is often moving in the air as the player takes his cut, and the player must focus his attention on the incoming pass, possibly as they are moving towards it, and hitting the window at the proper angle. It is no easy task at high speed.

So, it must be practiced. Each player can and should learn the skill of catching a pass at three points after it has been passed and while it is moving - the inside lane, the center lane, and the outside lane.

Drilling in this way forces a player to (1) keep light footed throughout his run; (2) turn exceedingly sharp without hesitation; and thus (3) reveal his decision to an unwitting defense at the very last moment.

There is a drill variation that helps with this.

▶ The setup of the drill is the classic "gauntlet" my university coach drilled us on:

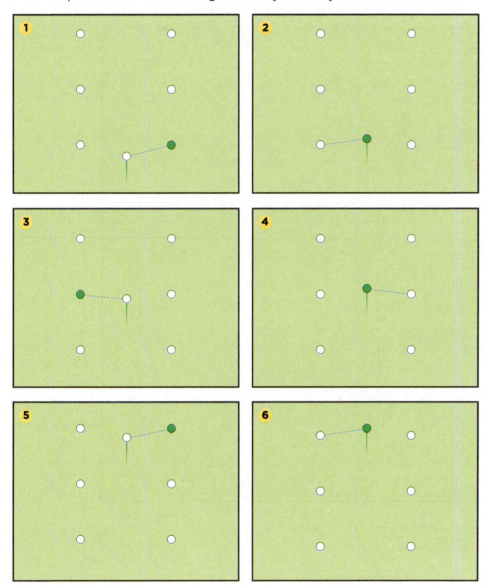

▶ The variation that makes a difference is requiring a sharp break at the third passing station. After two pass transfers on the center line, the attacker is forced to choose to catch the ball to the inside or the outside:

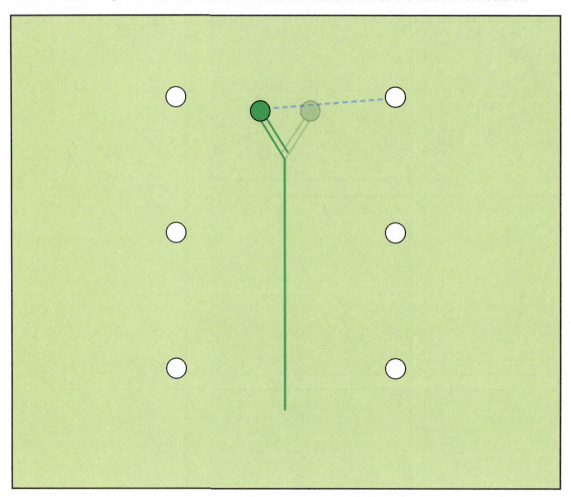

▶ A player or coach can progress the drill by adding a defender. A defender at the third station would likewise force a reception to the outside or inside lane, respectively. The drill can be further expanded by widening the drill, then adding attacking players who must transfer the ball from one side to the other in succession, quickly and accurately.

This drill adds critical skill depth to the receiving ball carrier's game, allowing them to enhance their performance in the 2 v. 2 drill variation, below. While reading defender movement, the second attacker will have better timing, know how to step into a pass or away from it, and place dizzying pressure on defenders.

Speed and timing are key. Once mastered, the above skill represents an element that enhances any offensive game.

PHIL'S TIPS...

"Reduce the width of playing zone to increase pressure in practice. Over time, you see the results:
Develop blue thinking, which is made while calm and with time to make a good decision.
Reduce red thinking, which is pressured and panicked thinking without time to react."

Drill 2:
Establishing Field Vision and Complex Attacking, All in One.

▶ Applying the catalogue of tactics in this book requires live practice that artificially sets the conditions necessary to win.

However, practice must be as close to real as possible, and there must be a chance for an offense player to fail if they do not act quickly and precisely.

Why? So that when a player sees the real thing, they are ready.

I long considered that the simple 2 v. 1 drill was the best at recreating the conditions of play. The defending player tosses the ball the offensive set to start the play, each has an equal distance to run around a cone to enter the playing area, and speed and precision decides the winner. The offense is naturally favored with a numerical advantage in hand and simply needs to execute on their advantage.

But live play doesn't always present that situation. Coaching a winning attack philosophy means teaching players how to break the tackle line in a 2 v. 2 and 3 v. 2 situation. A much more complicated prospect.

I thought to myself, "What if I could teach a player to break the window on a crash like I teach them how to pin a single defender in a 2 on 1 situation?" If I could do that, I might be able to teach "field vision," which would be a boon to growing each player into a threatening attacker, both on and off the ball.

So I altered the 2 v. 1 drill. In developing the modified drill, I considered "field vision" as the ability to gather information to plan and deploy an attack. Attacking players need to see the defenders. See which ones are out of place. Which are cheating. Which are lazy. Then the attackers could exploit those defenders. Field vision would be a form of pattern recognition, analysis, and execution that comes with practice and dedication.

This modified drill requires players to look at the defense. I knew that a player could fail to achieve field vision if only for failing to take the time to look at the opposing defense. I saw this flaw in my game, particularly early in my playing career. As a coach, I saw it in most players, even some veterans, and most certainly the young players. It is simply terrifying for some players to eye the defense considering the intensity of the game. Players often believe that, by looking, they might reveal their attack plans. A player may otherwise be so singularly focused on receiving or carrying the ball that they fail to look. This spoils tactics.

The modified drill also allows a player to memorize attack shapes and their movements. A player can fail to achieve field vision for failure to know and execute the attacks in this book. Some players do look at the defense, see it, but don't have the tools to respond. They have not read Break the Line (First or Second Edition), do not have several attack shapes in mind, and so getting information on the defense is useless. They cannot apply a method to solve the problem they are facing. Their analysis has no purpose. This nullifies potential.

Players and coaches should thus use the 2 v. 1 drill, with some tweaks to make it a 2 v. 2 and 2 v. 3 drill, to tease out the skill of analyzing defenses and executing attacks. The end result should make "field vision" a teachable skill, unlocking the potential of each player to move and react to the defense, and increase the chances that during live play an attack will break the line.

▶ Most all players and coaches are familiar with the following, and should use it regularly:

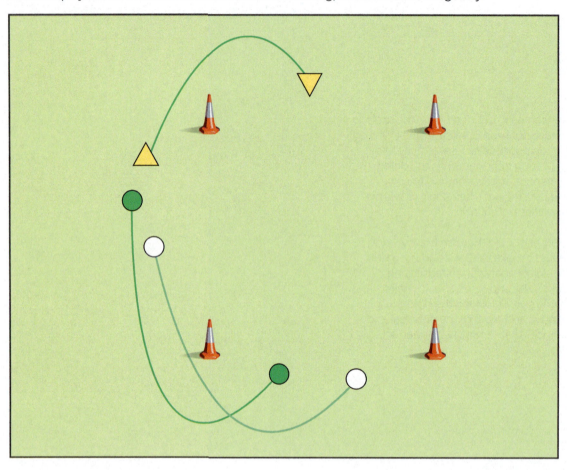

▶ This is the traditional drill.

Players should be (1) racing to get to the tackle line; (2) operate at full speed if possible; and (3) incorporate movements pre-tackle line.

All of the details matter. The movement towards the inside lane by the ball carrier threatens the inside lane and holds the defender in this drill, just as it would a match. The defender needs to turn his shoulder to address the threat by the ball carrier, and at that point, is out of position to reach the second attacker even in the event that the defender anticipates the pass.

Players often run through this drill lazily, without that detail. That's why each repetition needs to be critiqued with a short comment called out from the coach – "good" / "slow" / "lazy" / "nice!" – so that players get feedback on their performance and know when they've done wrong.

Later in the season, losses by the offense should be met with direct and immediate coaching correction.

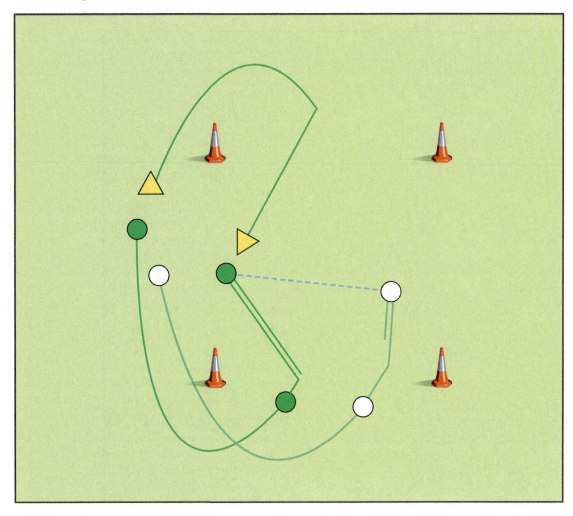

▶ To tease out crashing skills, use this same methodology with two defenders and add a delay cone around which the second defender must run:

▶ This will create the imbalance necessary for the drill. Just as with the 2 v. 1 drill, players will be rewarded for attacking and defending with speed, with the natural advantage going to the offense. The second attacker should be encouraged to radically angle to catch the pass, do everything to avoid the second defender, and then worry about straightening later.

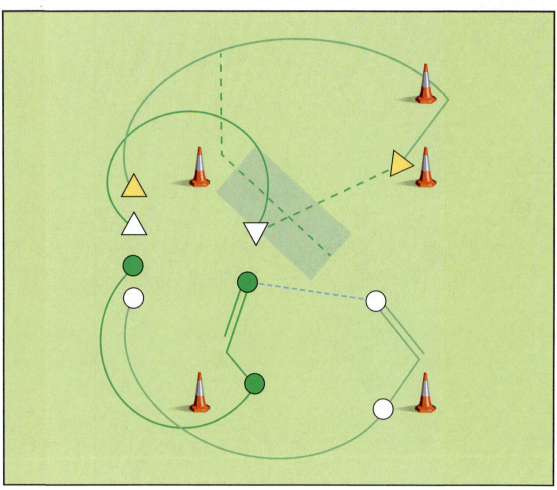

Drills

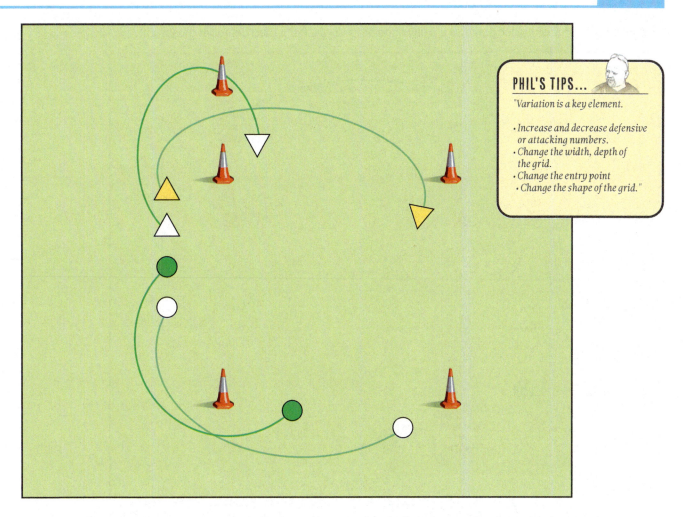

PHIL'S TIPS...

"Variation is a key element.

- *Increase and decrease defensive or attacking numbers.*
- *Change the width, depth of the grid.*
- *Change the entry point*
- *Change the shape of the grid."*

▶ A delayed first defender mixes it up. The ball carrier oftentimes simply keeps the ball. However, instruct the first defender to chase the second, making the scissor option the proper attack.

The ball carrier can then learn that he must keep one eye on the defender, the other on his oncoming help. He can then make the decision that leads to the winning attack.

▶ To tease out complex option play, use a delay cone around which the third defender must run:

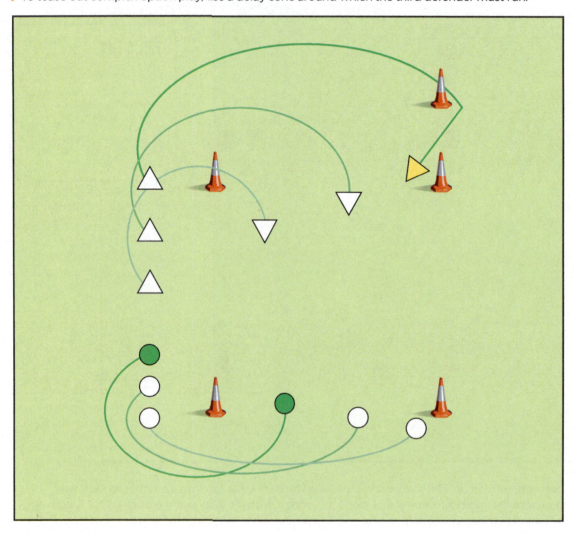

- Players will initially struggle with the delay cone. But allow the drill to run naturally. The delayed defender should be straining to reach his defensive position and be - by virtue of distance - unable to make a perfect defensive line unless the offense is exceedingly slow.

- When players are feeling confident, increase the complexity. This drill drives home the fact that any situation can be dissected. It should be run with plenty of space to accommodate even six or seven players. The offense should be given the advantage. The onus of coordinating the attack should not be distributed, but left primarily with the first attacker.

- A variation on this drill changes which defensive player is the weak defensive player. This can be done by forcing all players to start with their backs to the play area, then changing the cone position to delay one or more defensive players.

- In all of these modified attacking drills, there is an incentive for the offensive players to examine the defects in a given defense. By having even numbers, the offensive players must find aspects of the defense other than numerical advantage. The offense must learn to identify delays, over aggressiveness, and other weaknesses that may present themselves. And they must coordinate the speed and timing of their attack. The drill variation helps with all of that.

The same drills are also marvelous at ridding most players of their hesitance in breaking the tackle line. The concept is naturally foreign to many players. The angles seem extreme and at times counter intuitive. But with this drill variation, a player can get comfortable with seeing the window in repetition. That same player can then get accustomed to breaking it without hesitation.

Breaking the window, and thus the tackle line, comes with a certain feel that encompasses the speed and attention necessary to catch the ball during a pressure-filled attack. It is an intense, incredible feeling. The more a player can feel that feeling, the more they can grow accustomed to it, the more their nerves will hold when the time is right.

Naturally, coach and player can start these "equal numbers" drills as a touch drill. But the real progress comes when the drill is a contact drill, and players feel the approach of the defense and take the angles necessary to defeat the defense.

The drill need not be limited to even numbers attacking. Every single attacking situation in this book can be plugged into this drill, with cones to disable and create defects in the line of the defense. Coaches and players should endeavor to simulate every situation in this book, and therefore communicate that each attacking scenario can be won by the offense.

The drill, if set up properly, allows the offense to break the line not just in practice, but in games.

Conclusion 6

With attention to detail and discipline, you can break the tackle line as a player or coach.

Since rugby is a thinking player's game, that must include learning about the why and the how of executing the most exciting maneuvers of the game. The ideas included here should give you the fresh edge necessary to excel in the game of rugby.

When the tactics start bearing fruit, you should see a few things change on your team. Your team will start making breakaways. You should see better attacks in the loose and in set plays. And your team may in fact begin to trust backline plays whenever they're called.

If the tactics produce a stalemate with your opponent, worry not. Well-run tactics still place pressure on the weakest parts of a defense and promise to "break the dam" late in a match.

Good tactics will also keep your team fresh. A team that continually and repeatedly applies precise tactics will maintain possession and use energy in the most efficient way possible relative to the defense.

The tactics will then impact your game strategy. Building a game strategy based on these tactics gives your team additional chances to use the elements of attack to score, and therefore win.

So get out there and make it happen.

Learn the elements.

Practice the tactics.

Implement your strategy.

Break the line!

Like Break the Line: Second Edition?

Leave a review on Amazon.com!

The popularity of this book depends on reader reviews!

**Follow us on
Instagram and Twitter for more!
@BTLrugby**

Printed in Great Britain
by Amazon